Audre Lorde Knows What I Mean — 2021 in review

Audre Lorde Knows What I Mean — 2021 in review

A Poetry Collection

AC Benus

an AC Benus Impression
San Francisco

Grateful acknowledgement is here offered
for the support and encouragement
I've received on the literary site
www.gayauthors.org.

ISBN 978-1-953389-19-0 (ebook)
ISBN 978-1-953389-18-3 (paperback)

AUDRE LORDE KNOWS WHAT I MEAN — 2021 IN REVIEW:
A COLLECTION OF POEMS.
Copyright © 2022 by AC Benus.

Cover photo:
Pexels.com – Karolina Grabowska

Vignette:
Marbleized endpapers from an 1849 American monograph

Library of Congress Control Number: 2022902678

Foreword

This work is a follow-up of "Summer 2020 – Hell in a Handbasket" (San Francisco 2020), and one I had no intentions of writing. However . . . however, then January 6th occurred and made this new collection an inevitability.

As I did for the earlier, companion book of this one, I make no apology for the material you are about to encounter being "raw." These poems, largely written *eodem tempore* with when the news item referred to was unfolding, were prompted by a genuine wellspring of emotion. Yet, each of these inspiring moments was instantly tempered through the rigors of poetical form. Through this means of expression, I have confidence the words you're about to encounter will reflect the same thoughts and feelings you experienced. This then is the ugly year that was, 2021.

ACB

¤{ }¤{ }¤{ }¤{ }¤
¤{ }¤{ }¤{ }¤
¤{ }¤{ }¤
¤{ }¤

January 6, 2021

A crime that robs one of sleep in the night;
A spot that won't come out – turns oceans blood –
Steals the clear thinking needed to indict
With hands above hyperbole and mud.
For being indignant might harm one's case
And wind up supporting the sham defense
Justifying wrongs with smiles on the face,
While deafening blind justice with pretense.
But the crime's magnitude robs all of sleep
With stains enough to turn the Green One red,
As the pulse of our republic runs deep
And by a cruel assassin has been bled.
*   Angry's the voice that in this I now raise,*
*   Knowing righteous ire too deserves its praise.* [1]

Part One: Past as Prologue
From a Time of Plague I

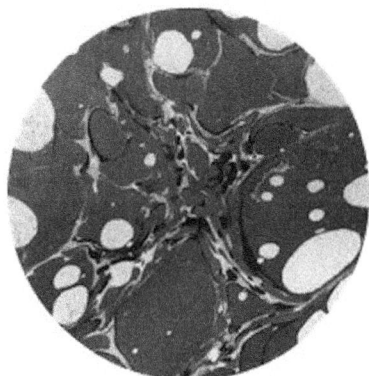

*"God offers to every mind
its choice between truth and repose.
Take which you please—*

—you can never have both."
—Ralph Waldo Emerson
1840s [2]

I.

Remember the Maine
Remember Pearl Harbor
Remember 9/11—
Remember January 6th.

Each one, except one,
Was a foreign attack –
A force outside our land –
Except one led by Donald Trump.

Remember One-Six
Remember all the lies
Remember the Gops did it
Remember January 6th. [3]

II.

Forgive and forget?
  Fuck that.
Move on, they say,
  The criminals,
To which we all say
  Fuck that
  & Fuck you—
Rot in jail and see if
The Dumpster,
For whom you broke
The rule of the Constitution,
  Will do a thing to
Even pretend he gives
  A shit about you,
You idiots, you Gops.
  Fuck that
  & Fuck you. [4]

III.

What Bozos – those who ranked The Dumpster
The Fourth Worst president in history—
Attempting to complete their summary
Of his inactions and ineptitudes
Before the January 6th razzamatazz
Could change their minds in a blinding hurry.

> *But think how short is public memory*
> *When a natural-born loser has,*
> *Like Dump, not even the evil energy*
> *To be ranked the barrel-scraped*
> *Worst humanity's ever seen . . .*

But then again, the scholars' work
Was premature, and they set the bar
Lower than even the lowest benchmark
The Nation has ever imagined
For someone being a so-called president—
Before the January 6th razzamatazz. [5]

IV.

If past is prologue, what is the present?—
Who from the point of time a few years back
Could have guessed the debasement of attack
The have-it-alls would use as argument:
"To Hell with free votes – trust Gops or repent
Your *sin* of not believing we'd highjack
Your rights with a megalomaniac!"
So if the prologue's past, what's the present?—
      On January 6th, their Party flew
      America as a jetliner in
      The Ground Zero of democracy.

Yet everyone in the past always knew
The Repubs would do our country in
Through greed and their own mediocracy.

V.

If there's a hope in this world, it might come
Believing every dog will have his day,
And the Big Lie supporters must succumb
To facing the Truth, no matter what they say.
Let them come to find out how they were used—
Their taxes raised; *their* healthcare corrupted;
Their religions mocked; *their* racism abused
To have *our* freedoms rolled back; undid.
So I'm glad their kids laugh in their faces,
Knowing they'll never vote Republican,
For it's a cult of Hate with no places
For decent folks, their realities or kin.
    The only hope is, it's gotten this bad,
    And they made their own children fucking mad. [6]

VI.

Ballade

Septimius Severus lives in my song –
The Roman emperor who turned lunatic,
Hater of laws, proponent of every wrong,
Who used the mob to brawl for his every trick
And tear down their own nationhood brick by brick –
But my *Severus* a modern country baits
Into murderous-suicide politic;
Rome didn't survive; will the United States?

Though of different times, both weaponize the throng,
And if Severus knew more of rhetoric,
The loud Gops simply know how to prolong
The confusion they've sprinkled like arsenic
In the minds of their rabble, whose skulls are thick
And can never keep track of the facts or dates
Their Party's leaders sing and dance like a schtick;
Rome didn't survive; will the United States?

The Emperor's accomplishments? Diving headlong
Into a ruined economy; Benedict
Arnolds made of former patriots once strong,
But grabbing all they could for themselves, and quick,
'Fore everything fell apart under that prick
Spreading beneath him a plethora of hates
For liberty, justice, anything not sick –
Rome didn't survive; will the United States?

Envoi

So, you – modern reader – will you be maverick
And resist the current Severus who waits
To destroy all, once and for all, just for a kick –
Rome didn't survive; will the United States? [7]

¤{ }¤{ }¤{ }¤{ }¤
¤{ }¤{ }¤{ }¤
¤{ }¤{ }¤
¤{ }¤

Part Two: A Society Awash in Anger

Social Justice I

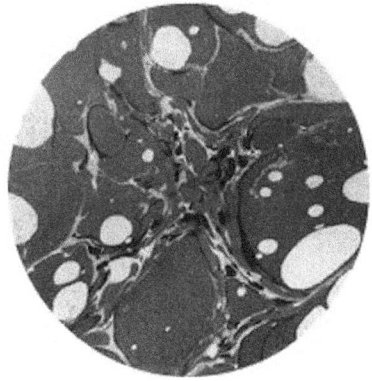

*"The mind of a bigot
is like the pupil of the eye –*

*The more light you pour upon it,
the more it will contract."*

—Oliver Wendell Holmes, [8]
circa 1882

VII.

A consequence-based community
   Is what the cynical Gop talkingpoint
Known as 'Cancel Culture' truly is.

Are not kindergarteners taught that
   Breaking the societal compact gets punished?
And yet, somehow, Repubs are excused?

Keep up the hypocrisy, A-holes,
   And see retribution-based politics
Send your Party the way of the dodo.

VIII.

Anger;
Righteousness
'Gainst racial wrongs
Treated as the norm –
Enrage

Why then
Just pretend
Business as usual's
The best we get
Sleeping?

Rise up,
Or sit down,
Civil obedience, or not –
A fist in the air
Symbol

Freedom
From the lies;
That's all we ask –
The end of othering
For all.

IX.

John Sullivan, Utah progressive,
Was treated differently from the others
Who stormed the Capitol on January 6th –
While the true Trump-head seditionists
Got Gop-court-ordered slaps on the wrist,
Sullivan, charged mere hours after arrest,
Faced 5-years in prison felonies –
So I ask you a simple question:
Can you guess the color of his skin? [9]

X.

Segregation dead in Louisiana,
  Or the dead segregated in that state?

    January, 2021 – more than 20 years
    Into the new century – and a deputy sheriff's
    Family is refused his burial in the
    Oaklin Springs cemetery, because the
    Board insists Blue Lines don't matter
    Over the 'n_gr_' status of one of their
    Fallen. No. No Blacks allowed in
    Sacred, white soil, no matter who the soul
    Might be; no matter that it's 20 fucking
    Years into a new century tired as fuck
    With all this 19th century bullshit.

Segregation dead in Louisiana . . . ?
  No, the dead segregated in that state. [10]

XI.

Isolated; Random –
That's all "They" ever say –
The Media, the Cops, the FBI,
The Schoolboards, the Cop Unions,
The Mayors, the Supervisors, the
Bum-fucked Anybodies excusing
Inexcusable Homophobia, Racial Bias,
Sexism, Gender-Shaming, and On and On –
"Nothing to see here, folks, our
     Company's . . .
     President's . . .
     Nation's . . .
     Queen's . . .
     District's . . .
     Officer's . . .
     Town's . . .
     Country's . . .
     Pope's . . .
     County's . . .
     Leader's . . .
     Prince's . . .
     Sheriff's . . .
     Admin's . . .
     Secretary . . .
     Prime Minister's . . .
     Attorney's . . .
     King's . . .
     Representative's . . .
     Alderman's . . .
     Senator's . . .
     Lord's . . .
     Bishop's . . .
     Anything at All's . . .
Bigotry is just a Random one-off
Event. Nothing systemic to see here, so
Move along; move along."

XII.

What in our 'blessèd' world
   Could possibly be more 'Christian'
Than five instructors at the Saint Charles,
   Missouri, so-called "Christian High School"
Spelling out the word **"C-O-O-N"**
   At a harmless, blameless school picnic
Games competition? Nothing, according to the
   Schoolboard.

         No consequences –
         No firings; no reprimands;
         No sanctions; zero; zip, no costs
         For the flagrant bullying shown to
         The school's Black children.

"God bless, 'em. They're doing the Lord's Work"
   Is no doubt what this so-called 'Christian'
Schoolboard said behind closed doors. [11]

¤{ }¤{ }¤{ }¤{ }¤
¤{ }¤{ }¤{ }¤
¤{ }¤{ }¤
¤{ }¤

Part Three: Swan Song
Environmental Collapse I

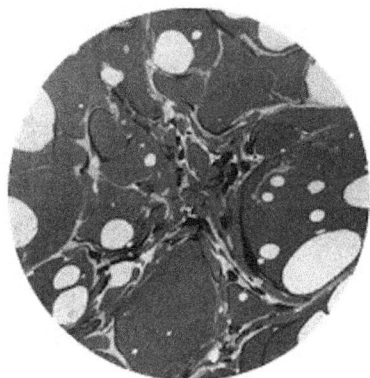

*"When I hear of the destruction of a species,
I feel as if all the works of some great writer
has perished."*

—Theodore Roosevelt,
February 15th, 1899 [12]

XIII.

Three Triolets on a Theme

i.

There is no freshness now left in the air
Because the wildfires have drenched it in smoke,
And over a land wasted in despair
There is no freshness now left in the air
And no one seems to even give a care
The world outside's forced to admit and choke
There is no freshness now left in the air
Because the wildfires have drenched it in smoke.

ii.

Open windows to outside air,
For it is stifling through and through
And ash will get in if you dare
Open windows to outside air,
Because the world burns everywhere—
So choose carefully if you do
Open windows to the outside air,
For it is stifling through and through.

iii.

Here there is no breath in today's foul air
   Which windows closed or open cannot hide,

     For death from the forest fires' dark lair
     Shows there is no breath in today's foul air
     Which strips the woods of life and leaves them bare

As warning that none should again reside
   Where there is no breath in today's foul air
Which windows closed or open cannot hide. [13]

XIV.

Twenty-three, the species declared extinct,
Greets an autumn headline when we awake.
They disappeared not all at once, but now,
There's some truth from D.C. on the Nation's
Environmental State of the Union.
It's a caught-up moment of sobering
Honesty for all to minimize,
Ignore, false-debate, deny, lie about
As our Big-Money Politics sees fit. [14]

XV.

Kyrielle

The young are without hope the Earth
    Can survive Man's heartless onslaught,
For if one surveys action's dearth,
    You know they feel just as they ought
        —And I, young at heart, am with them.

Everywhere they look, there's despair,
    While truth to tell, it's in their lungs
Breathing in the sulphurous air,
    Feeling it coating on their tongues
        —And I, young at heart, am with them.

For decades' worth of lip service
    Has done the world's children no good,
Except raise them sad and nervous
    Their kids will hate them as they should
        —And I, young at heart, am with them. [15]

XVI.

Little Willie

Willi thought everything was nice
    as he froze to death in the ice,
fumbling with his rosary beads
    as if life's a string of misdeeds.

XVII.

Why should I be shocked?—
And yet, I was.
A satellite view,
Of current times,
Clearly shows Brazil
As it is now—
A vast savanna
With rainforests
Completely wiped out.
There's nothing now,
Save some margins on
The Amazon's
Capillary banks.
But, do not fear—
They'll soon go as well,
For nothing stops
Mankind's slash and burn,
Though it's our flesh
His machete strikes;
Though it's our soul
His flames plow asunder. [16]

XVIII.

Biomass, Biomass, you can't compete
With the weight of all our manmade crap, so
Biomass, Biomass, toss us over
And let centrifugal force hurl us
Into the darkest Hell of our nightmares—
Biomass, Biomass, we can't survive. [17]

XIX.

How many have been the poems written
   On the soothing sanctity of the rain,
    And yet, in Greenland this year, it was rain
That witnessed the ice with drops be bitten.

For the first time in recorded history,
   Heat made it rain steadily on the snow
    And great cataracts of runoff to flow,
While the cause of it was no mystery.

Past the point of a shot across the bow,
   What this winter was, unprecedented,
    Will happen every year unprevented
As the 'way it is' in the here and now.

    No use to seek wisdom where'er it stands,
    For our doomsday strides unstopped through the lands. [18]

¤{ }¤{ }¤{ }¤{ }¤
¤{ }¤{ }¤{ }¤
¤{ }¤{ }¤
¤{ }¤

Part Four: The Fly
From a Time of Plague II

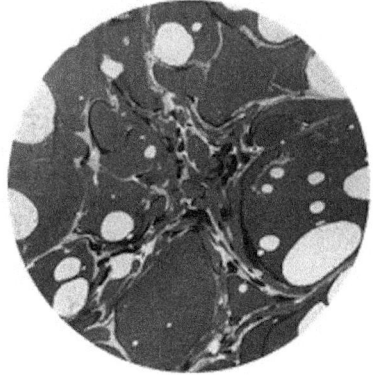

*"By gnawing through a dyke,
even a rat may drown a nation."*

—Edmund Burke,
circa 1759 [19]

XX.

The ultimate symbol of elitism,
    He even boasted with a glinting sneer
    That he could get away with mass murder.

As it stands now, it's even worse, for
    He's getting away with stabbing our way of life
    In the back like a pouting frat boy. [20]

XXI.

"Mitch McConnell; Mitch McConnell,
  Send your hypocrisy right over—
For your Fat-Cat money funnel
  Keeps 'forcing the city gates' we treasure
With your criminalities' pull
  To be our Constitution's betrayer."

XXII.

The Fly

the fly has arms
these arms go to the eyes
to wipe the slime
gathered there in filth

then slimy hands
go into the fly's mouth
so it can suck
the dirty into its soul

sputum; maggots
the Gop party infects
democracy's corpse
with their hatred

they think we're dead
that we have given up
and accept lies
as their par-for-the-course

but our freedom
has one last summer day
to fend off the rot
they've seeded deep in us

will we take it
take the slight time we have
to clean the wound,
or will we die?

XXIII.

Sestina

This then is the Gop's idea of kinder,
Their degenerated sense of gentler,
To ignore the police prone to murder,
To break bones, crush skulls in sustained mayhem
And rubber-stamp their wicked hearts depraved,
Knowing at root, the Party's a bully.

Every minority they now bully,
Making a mockery of their kinder
Words which nothing mean 'cept to the depraved
Who go out hunting for victims gentler
To shoot down in the street and drive mayhem
Like fear down the throat of random murder.

For who protects and serves when cops murder,
Knowing their whims are sheltered by bully
Tactics in Congress akin to mayhem
As the Gops filibuster laws kinder
To a beleaguered public whose gentler
Instincts get daily crushed by the depraved?

Their "Qualified Immunity's" depraved
When it leads to unjustified murder
Being cops' default position gentler
To say Blue Lives matter like a bully,
Never once thinking how to be kinder
When their one weapon is public mayhem.

When the public wants an end to mayhem,
They have nowhere to go that's not depraved;
No hand to seek that's actually kinder
From a force that's unconcerned with murder
At the hands of one it knows is a bully,
But keeps on the street to become gentler.

So, hollow the Gops' words about *gentler,*
When for political ends, it's mayhem
They promote with the fear of a bully

That knows nothing but how to be depraved,
Turning blind eyes to organized murder
And call brutality their kind of *kinder*.

Envoi

So where's your kinder; how about your gentler?
Do you want murder; do you need mayhem
To stay this depraved and act the bully? [21]

XXIV.

What could be more *hateful* in this country
Than the two Jim Crow tools the Gops protect?—
Which spit in the face of the Land of the Free
With contempt for those they do not respect.

> Their Filibuster's used to oppress some,
> While the Electoral College maintains
> The *white* few rule the many for years to come,
> No matter who wins election campaigns.
> The Senate minority wields power
> To see that 30% 'NO!' votes win
> To make The People's agenda cower
> 'Neath Big-Money politics' ugly grin.

What could be more *racist* in this nation
Than the Jim Crow hacks the Gops use to sway?—
Which they wield as sledge-hammer damnation
On Truth, Justice – the American Way. [22]

XXV.

Villanelle

"Now, can you guess the color of their skin . . . "
Cries out a guilty national conscience,
Knowing it's our true original sin.

For beneath absolution's origin
Curls the poison, viper-like Judas hiss
"Now, can you guess the color of their skin . . . "

And self-hatred has no self-discipline
In its arbitrary nature's compass,
Knowing it's our true original sin.

'Cause cornered venom like adrenalin
Bites the words of their victims' forgiveness
"Now, can you guess the color of their skin . . . "

So what future is there to imagine
Where we'll be able to overcome this,
Knowing it's our true original sin.

Although past and present are maudlin,
They're nothing compared to the future's abyss—
"Now, can you guess the color of their skin . . . "
Knowing it's our true original sin.

XXVI.
The question
At one time used to be
How can we work the best together

To enhance our tremendous opportunities
As a nation pulling as a team,
Setting squabbles aside
As minor.

And yet now
One Party's made rancour
Their 'get out the vote' mainstay of hate,
Hissing like the snake in our Garden of Eden
That 'the others' are coming for you,
So against self-interest,
Vote Repub.

Lies, lies, lies,
And privately funded
Propaganda's how they stay in charge,
Deceiving worst those who can ill afford their greed,
Syphoning their taxes for the rich
In bait and switch, smoke-screen
Politics.

So I ask,
What will remove the plank
From their ever splinter-seeking eyes,
When they're lied to and deceived by Republicans,
Who only con folks in their blindness
To follow them to Hell,
And like it.

¤{ }¤{ }¤{ }¤{ }¤
¤{ }¤{ }¤{ }¤
¤{ }¤{ }¤
¤{ }¤

Part Five: Fair Questions for Now

Social Justice II

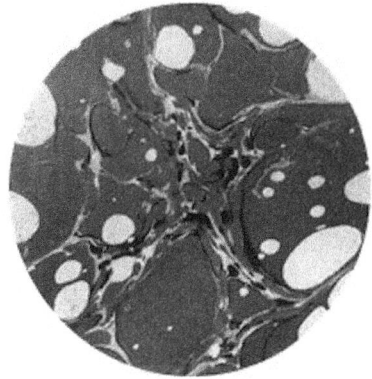

"The [African American] says, 'Now.'
    Others say, 'Never!'
The voice of responsible
    Americans . . . we say, 'Together.'"
                    —Lyndon Baines Johnson,
                        May 30th, 1963 [23]

XXVII.

Let's play a game, shall we?—
　Called Work Out the Color of Their Skin.

　　First, let's look at N. B.—
　　　Ten-year-old girl bullied at school
　　By another student.
　　　She draws a picture of said bully;
　　Then bully's parents call,
　　　Demanding the child be arrested.
　　What did school and cops do?
　　　Throw her in a room by herself,
　　Sans the girl's mom,
　　　And then proceed to bully
　　By interrogation.
　　　Then they handcuff her; perp-walk her
　　For her classmates to see;
　　　Take her to the County Jail
　　And lock her behind bars.
　　　So, Surmise the Color of N. B.'s Skin.

　　What about Luke Stewart?—
　　　Whose parents will always regret
　　Calling the cops to help
　　　Locate the twenty-three-old.
　　For the cops sure found him,
　　　Sleeping peacefully in his car.
　　What did the two cops do?—
　　　One chokes him, trying to drag him
　　Out from behind the wheel,
　　　While the other got in the car,
　　Tased the young man six times,
　　　After punching the hell out of him,
　　Then killed with five bullets.
　　　All within **60** seconds' span
　　From first police assault

To Stewart's last moments on Earth.
Luke's parents know you can
Deduce the Color of their Son's Skin. [24]

XXVIII.

A Ballade's perfect refrain might go:
"What has happened to the Peace of long ago?"

And it seems a fair question, for now,
While we cast our glance about and wonder how

Things were ever let get this bad,
With the Republicans stealing all we had

Of equality's fair momentum,
Replaced with brutalities ugly and dumb.

So the relevant refrain must go:
"What has happened to the Peace of long ago?"

XXIX.

No happy endings; no happy endings—
Matthew Rhodes – white cop
Louis Catalani – white cop
The killers of Luke Stewart
In Euclid, Ohio, in 2017 will never
Face the just punishment for cold-blooded
Killing because the Gop's
'Qualified Immunity' ensures
Cold-blooded killers remain in
Uniform, just as
Matthew Rhodes – white cop
Louis Catalani – white cop
Continue to prowl the streets
Of Euclid, Ohio, to this day. [25]

XXX.

Guess the color of Kyle Rittenhouse's judge
    Who will not allow in his courtroom
    For the protesters Kyle shot and killed on video
    The decency of being referred to as "victims"
    By the prosecution? White.

Guess the color of Ahmaud Arbery's jury
    In the trial of the men who lynched
    Him with a shotgun on a Georgia road
    And were not indicted for a crime
    For the longest time? White. [26]

XXXI.

Audre Lorde knows what I mean.
Decades ago now, she wrote a poem
About a 37-year-old cop standing in the blood
Of the 10-year-old he'd fatally shot
With the words "Die, you little motherfucker!"
Slutting his lips of vile hate; devilish malice.

Audre Lorde knows what I mean.
Decades ago now, she wrote a poem
About a jury of 11 whites intimidating the slight
Twelfth Black woman into acquitting the cop who'd
Killed a little boy because he was Black,
And boasted about it on the witness stand with vile hate.

And how that cop was free to do it again;
And how Lorde, as a Gay Woman, could expect
No support from the Black community – no love –
Simply because her partner was a white woman;
Because no victim of oppression, they said,
Is free of the taint of where they're perceived to come from.

Audre Lorde knows what I mean.
Decades ago she penned a poem
About death and hatred; about prejudice on her
As a Gay person full of love, but fed to the teeth with anger
And the righteous Need to do what little one can
To put wrongs right. She wrote about me. [27]

XXXII.

A November Tanka

My day rises cold
with a strange light in the air;
nandina ripen
like blood splatter on the wind,
asking when clear light might shine. [28]

¤{ }¤{ }¤{ }¤{ }¤
¤{ }¤{ }¤{ }¤
¤{ }¤{ }¤
¤{ }¤

Part Six: Fait Accompli
Environmental Collapse II

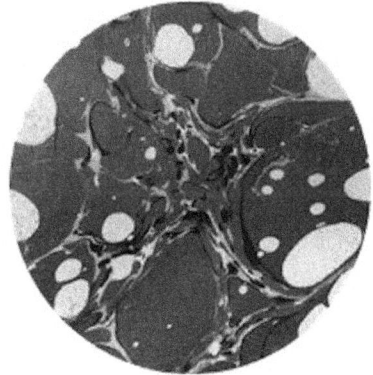

"It is not always
'the other person'
who pollutes our streams,
or litters our highways,
or throws away a match in a forest –

– or wipes out game –
– or wipes out our fishing reserves."
—John F. Kennedy,
September 24th, 1963 [29]

XXXIII.

Again, a look outside
Produces the sight of
A strange miasma
In the air.

Wood ash, diesel pollution,
Fog from the sea
All mix sadness and despair
In the air.

Morning's First Glimpse,

Spet. 6th, 2021 [30]

XXXIV.

The kitchen table is clean,
Its wood shining as pat as human will –
But in a mere day or two
A layer looking like the worst
Neglect of a year of no dusting
Collects and dulls its brightness,
Almost as if before my watching eyes –
My only too human eyes.

Only

    – It's not dust at all.
     It's forest fire ash. It's the
     Climate collapse
     Collecting before
     My only too human eyes. [31]

XXXV.

How out of touch are we –
 Surprised by every drought
 Surprised by every flooding.

Meanwhile, people drown in
 Subway cars in China
 And nearly in New York too.

Meanwhile, reservoirs in the West
 So low, hydroelectric generators
 Are silent for the first time in 100 years.

How out of touch are we –
 Surprised by the reality of 2021
 Surprised at how bad we'll let things become. [32]

XXXVI.

Glasgow 2021 – Climate Summit –
 Gimme a break – what a farce
 What a display of hypocrisy.

  Hypocrisy of the Queen addressing the conference
  When She's opted out her vast "Royal" lands
  In Scotland from any – tepid – environmental regulation.
  The crownèd grouse who's asserted her "right"
  To be self-governing, which makes her 100%
  The same as tyrants in Russia, China, Brazil.
  The Opt-Out Option has already killed the world.

So what's the purpose of Glasgow 2021 –
 Climate Summit – when it's a farce
 And a strutting display of hypocrisy. [33]

XXXVII.

It was nearly 20 years ago now
Lil Bushy Junior stood before Congress
And slurred: "'Merica's addicted to
Furran oyle!" And what's happened?

The real problem is, America's addicted
To "Good News," no matter what dire
Truths may lurk in the blight light
Of reality-based reality.

  Our dependency on
  "Success Stories" – is to blame.
     – Like *ozone control,* when
       There are two holes, not just
       The one of 1980s concern, for now
       Both North and South points have rotted away.
     – Like the *whales are saved,* when here
       Japan and the Norway hunt and slaughter
       More than ever, Japan with impunity
       In Australian-declared "Protected" waters.
     – Like the *rainforests are safe,* when now
       It doesn't matter. In Brazil, in the
       Last 15 years, they've all been slashed and burned
       While we watched; right before our eyes.

Such "Success Stories" may ease
Stupid consciences in fat countries
But will be the death of the world
Through "Feel Good" Addictions
And "XYZ are Saved!" dependencies. [34]

XXXVIII.

For the ecological year
    That was 2021 – a headline
Somehow can make it clear:

> *"Blizzard warnings issued for*
> *Hawaii with a least 12 inches of*
> *Snow forecast."*

Perhaps future eyes reading this
    Won't make such a fuss – after all
They may see it and think nothing's amiss. [35]

XXXIX.

Insect collapse, it's a *fait accompli,*
And if you don't believe me, look and see –
Birds around the world, dying in their droves.

And up next for the great cull that will be,
A third of fresh-water fish, fancy free,
Will starve as we sit and watch them decompose.

Not a third *en masse,* but a panoply
Of every species has a guarantee
To go the way of the extinct dodos.

So this *lai* I sing, for you must agree
The death sentence Man issues by decree
Is on Himself, while stupid people doze. [36]

¤{ }¤{ }¤{ }¤{ }¤
¤{ }¤{ }¤{ }¤
¤{ }¤{ }¤
¤{ }¤

Part Seven: "Damn Him"; "Damn You"; "Damn Me"

From a Time of Plague III

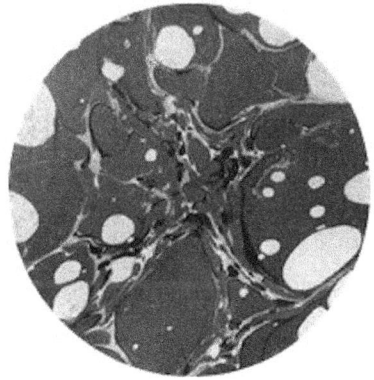

"The doctrine of
'The Strong shall Dominate the weak'
Is the doctrine of our enemies!
And we reject it."

—Franklin Delano Roosevelt,
December 24th, 1943 [37]

XL.

A BRIDGE TO THE 22ND CENTURY

Five Cinquains:

i.

His lies
Normalized lies,
Sicced a mob on Congress,
Set a cancer deep in our blood
To rot.

ii.

What shame
He brought to our kids;
Disgraced through all the years
They'll grow without democracy,
Enslaved.

iii.

Ideas
Kill much quicker
Weaponized and tempered
In the blood of true patriots,
Murdered.

iv.

Big lies
Are Gops' new norm –
Anything for power
And the taint of corporate money
To kill.

v.

What shame
We must live through,
Knowing they are plotting
To turn back every election
To win. [38]

XLI.

One-Party rule is what
    Karl Rove promised
        And the people let slip
           Into place.

Damn Him; Damn You; Damn Me. [39]

XLII.

Kyrielle
"Lord have mercy . . . "

Now each Gop-controlled state boldly employs
Voter suppression, with vote-stealing noise
On how "the others" stuff and cheat the count,
Knowing Repubs steal the largest amount,
    For fair fights they can't tolerate, it's true—
    Losers never can; bullies never do.

Like those insecure on the playground sands
Who intimidate anyone who stands
'Tween the blameless and what they want to steal,
They push others to the ground under heel,
Mewing how they're the ones made to suffer
As if the weak are really the tougher,
    For fair fights they can't tolerate, it's true—
    Losers never can; bullies never do.

Look at Hervis Rogers, arrested by
Texas Gops who claimed his race went awry
When he thought Black men could vote fair and free
In a State that screams *that* must never be –
The laws exist for the elite to say
Who can and can't vote on election day;
And now Gops expand this to every place
To make of freedom a crime and disgrace,
  For fair fights they can't tolerate, it's true—
  Losers never can; bullies never do. [40]

XLIII.

We didn't know how good we had it
before the plague of Covid;
before the plague of Trump.

And do you know what?
 before the plague of Covid
Both are still wreaking havoc,
 before the plague of Trump
both still doing damage afresh.

We didn't know how good we had it
 both are still wreaking havoc,
before the plague of Covid,
 both still doing damage afresh.
before the plague of Trump.

XLIV.

 Hervis Rogers was made
  An example:
   "Your vote doesn't matter,
    Black people."

Bless Him; Bless You; Bless Me.

XLV.

January 20, 2021

Inaugural Day, and no mention of *us* –
Not from the President;
Not from the Invocationalist, priest;
Not from the Benedictionalist, reverend . . .
    Unless, *we,* a strong, persecuted
    Minority who've faced burning at
    The stake; we, who've been enslaved
    By the iron band of hateful conformity;
    We, who've been spat upon by minister
    And priest alike in this so-called
    "Free" country – jailed, castrated,
    Institutionalized over and over and over and
    Over again based on their false
    Authority to 'speak' for God in tongues
    Of fire to damn *us* with each and
    Every malicious thought in their
    Sex-addled brains . . . unless, we
    Accept this Benedictionalist's reverend's *LABEL*
    Of people of a "preference."
So, no. *I* was not mentioned at the
Inaugural, January 20, 2021 . . . . [41]

XLVI.

    It's something any seven-year-old in this country
    Can understand. Winning; losing; being a victor;
    Being the defeated. Our culture makes sure
    Every American seven-year-old knows the sting of
    Dodge-ball losing; the losership of being picked
    Last for any and all activities of competitiveness.
    So when my Second Grade teacher, one fine
    Morning, looked so sad she could cry, standing

With folded hands in front of us – her Second
Grade class – to tell us America had
Done something it had never done before: Lost
A war. Saigon had fallen in spectacular way to a
Communist dictatorship, and helicopters were
Landing as precariously as butterflies atop the
U.S. embassy in Vietnam to rescue and ferry the
Good Guys – the ones who had fought to keep
Their nation a democracy – to safety and exile,
We, the Second Grade class of Saint John the
Baptist Elementary School got it. America, the
Loser, had lost a war. Its first in one hundred
and ninety-nine years of existence.
We seven-year-olds looked at each other knowing
The world had changed that morning; changed
To the detriment of all those who might
Struggle against dictatorship around the globe.
We didn't have to grapple with grand concepts;
We'd been reared to instantly understand
There are winner and losers among us, and at
All costs – within bounds of 'fairness' – one must
Strive mightily to be a winner at all times.
But. America had lost its first war, and
The victims of this loss were struggling that very
Morning to survive somehow under conditions
Too brutal to be anything but real in 1975.

This year, who could have imagined only
Months ago, classrooms across the land filled
With new seven-year-olds watching the
Hand-wringing of their youthful teachers standing
Before their class, telling them – or, at least
Attempting to convey the horror – of America's
Losership. For only the second time in our
Two hundred forty-fifth year of existence, we lost
A war; a war against religious dictators
Whose only aim was to impose their will on a
Public kowtowed, confused and scared. And America?

What did we do to help? Nothing, except keep
Alive Donald J. Trump's official policy of
Playing Surrender Monkeys to the Taliban.
Now, back after the loser lost once again
In a national election, there were some very
Adroit commentaries appearing in some very
Adroit newspapers that the Dumpster's loser
Mindset was sabotaging the American People,
The American Republic – our way of life; our
Sense of life in a secure world; our very
Democracy – with Foreign Policy decisions aimed
To explode like assign time bombs once the
Nation was feeling good; feeling safer the nutjob
Was out of office and far removed were his
KFC-greased fingers from the levers of war and peace.
So when the public was feeling better under
Actual leadership; under an actual President,
The Dumpster-fire's IEDs would explode to hurt
A country Donald J. Trump always, actually, despised;
Clearly he hates us for our freedoms and way of life.
It went off. BOOM! A distracted Biden Administration,
Trying to stamp out the thousand other wildfires
The Gops had weaponized to burn down the
Entire nation before they were shut off from
Power by the will of The People, let
The Repubs' "Surrender Monkey to the Taliban"
Policy stand. What lengths the Gops will
Go to hurt anyone not their corporate owners –
The Enrons; the GMs of the world; the Chevrons –
Should be no surprise to anyone with eyes open
And watching the crisis-points around the world
They've fostered for the sheer 'fear value'
They can exert over the American electorate
Decade upon decade, upon decade (anyone
Remember the "Grave Communist Threat"
Reagan's subtropical isle of Granada supposedly
Posed to the price of milk within the Good
Ole U.S.A.? Anyone recall King Bush I using

A U.S. warship to fire point-blank into
Housing along Panama's shore, killing hundreds
– incinerating large swaths of that nation's capitol –
Killing people sitting down to dinner, murdered,
Burned to a crisp because the former CIA-Director-
Cum-lied-his-way-into-the-Presidency
With nothing but Willie Horton Panic, said two-
Bit dictator Manuel Noriega was somehow a
Major feel-bad threat to the price of gasoline
In the Good Ole U.S.A.?) Fear. Value. That's
The Repub's stock-in-trade, whether here at home
Or on shores far away where the "Others" live,
Salivating to make suburbia's life a tiny fraction
Of a millimeter's width less comfortable and
Pampered, and whiny-nosed with useless complaints
On "How hard life is for us here." These are the losers
Who actually shit on their ballots so losers
Like Donald J. Trump could wipe his ass
On the United States Constitution. We've seen how
Much he cares about the Law. Same with every Gop
Who stood behind that so-called man. And why?
Because ours is a country the Gop Party had always,
Actually, despised; Clearly they are a seething
Mass of hate for us and our freedoms; our way of life.
So, is it any wonder such a band of dodge-ball-
Stung narcissists would sabotage the good war –
Begun by accident by Lil Bushy II so he could get
To Iraqi oil – for selfish, uncaring political
Manipulation of an overworked, underpaid,
Undereducated, highly taxed Gop-voting public?
Yes; yes; yes – a million Iraqi dead in a war
The American Gop-voting public rubber-stamped
And vomited up a trillion dollars in debt
To hand Chevron and Exxon and British Petroleum
And Royal Dutch Shell oil-contracts to keep
Pollution off the charts around the world
Forever. So, yes. Trump played surrender monkey;
Biden fell for it, and classrooms around the world

Had teachers stand up before it, telling them
America had lost only its second war in history.

But the horrors, the horrors, the man falling from
A jetliner's wheel well just trying to live; just
Trying to escape the terrorist Taliban. The crush
Of thousands at Kabul airport trying, just
Trying to get their children and themselves out
Of harm's way because they had had the
Audacity of Hope to believe democracy in
Afghanistan mattered to anyone but them.
But they were wrong, and Biden himself turned weak
The moment he stood before cameras – with a
Uselessly determined grimace on his antique,
Baby Boomer features – to say if the
Afghans can't fight for themselves against an
Organized – China and Iran and Russia funded –
Terrorist group, there was nothing the American
People could do about it either. Except, of course,
There was. Because by this point, the few thousand
U.S. troops who had kept peace in the land easily
For a decade had tripled to nearly 10,000; so they
Very well, very easily could have held the
Country – because it's what the educated American
Voting electorate wanted; expected – but no,
Biden said Trump had played surrender
Monkey to terrorists and there was nothing he
Could do about it – poor, little weakling –
Except watch his television like the rest of us.
Watch as frozen bodies of Afghans were crowbarred
From wheel wells of evacuation planes landed at
Ramstein Air Base in Germany carrying evacuated
Kids and their parents from Kabul. No,
Nothing he could do, he said, but live up to
The sabotage plans laid like assigns' time-
Bombs under the Democratic Administration.
Nothing he could do but count the bodies
And billions of dollars lost in 20 years of violence

In Afghanistan meaning nothing but a return of
The Taliban and their soccer stadiums full
Of political prisoners, Christians, Queer people,
Mowed down with machineguns. Nothing. He.
Could. Do. He said.

It's something any seven-year-old in this country
Can understand. Winning; losing; being a victor;
Being the defeated. Our culture makes sure
Every American seven-year-old knows the sting of
Dodge-ball losing; the losership of being picked
Last for any and all activities of competitiveness.
America, the loser, had lost its second war
In two hundred forty-five years of existence, only
The first loss of Saigon was despite our
Actually fighting for it – for democracy in
Vietnam – but Kabul . . . . Kabul we lost
Because Donald J. Trump and his Repub collaborators
Decided to walk away from the Afghan people;
Elected to walk away for racist reasons of
"Brown People Don't Matter," and Joseph R. Biden,
Old, and confused, and befuddled by Gop evilness,
Agreed. Afghans lost; Americans lost; the world
Will never be as it was, despite the sky-high
Cost of milk and dino-juice now hobbling middle-
America. So, on that fresh morning only a few
Months ago now, those seven-year-olds looked
At each other knowing the world had changed that day.
It had altered to the detriment of all those
Who would struggle against dictatorship – at
Home and abroad – around the globe. Those kids
In their myriad classrooms didn't have to struggle
With grand concepts, for they'd been reared
In this country to instantly understand there are
Winners and losers among us, and at all costs –
To hell with 'fairness' in these Gop-ruined days –
One must strive mightily to be a winner at
All times. But America had lost its second war,

And the victims of this loss were struggling that
Very morning to survive somehow under conditions
Too brutal to be anything but real in **2021.** [42]

¤{ }¤{ }¤{ }¤{ }¤
¤{ }¤{ }¤{ }¤
¤{ }¤{ }¤
¤{ }¤

Part Eight: Random Acts of Harshness

Social Justice III

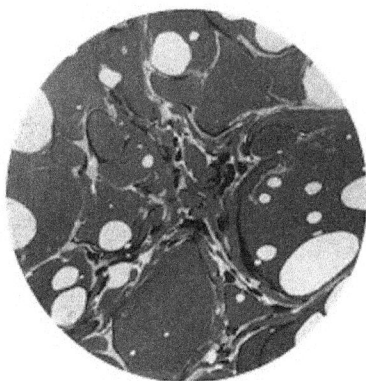

"We cannot be satisfied until all our people have equal opportunities for jobs, for homes, for education, for health, and for political expression; and until all our people have equal protection under the law."

—Harry S. Truman,
February 2nd, 1948 [43]

XLVII.

Random acts of harshness pervade,
    In this world we've let come to be,
And take the form, which by default,
    Seem most brutal for us to see.

Shotguns amid peaceful protests,
    Blood all over the pavement too,
Men murdered by a teenager
    More evil than they ever knew.

Random, older, women in cars,
    Flying into a rage when they
See BLM candle vigils,
    And plow right into them to slay.

Acts of smash and grab, no matter
    Neo-Nazi arson to blame
On peace-filled anti-fascist crowds,
    Or kids in jewelry stores – it's the same.

Random act of harshness allowed
    To strike dread in all and run free
Through a land where Reason is scorned,
    But Lord Mayhem rules by decree.

So, do we let the cities burn?—
    Call in the troops to enforce curfew?—
Fold our hands and pray for some calm
    When the God we've made has no clue

How the human heart makes caprice
    The very center of its fame,
Acting out in base randomness
    Because harshness is its only game. [44]

XLVIII.

"I want my dad!" is all the girl said,
    The 9-year-old, handcuffed,
    Already sitting in the back of
    A cop car, before she was pepper sprayed.

Not random acts of violence led bored,
    Uniformed, white-mom cop, to shake up
    The can of mace like a spray can
    Of paint, and with malice aforethought,
    Hurt the little girl under her sham title
    Of 'protection.'

"I want my dad!" and tears from a
    Scared little child, manhandled roughly,
    Brutally by white hands throwing her in
    The snow – "I want my dad!" So bad
    A crime, a third-grader "Required"
    To be traumatized for life by cops who
    Just wanted to get home to their own kids.

"Just spray her at this point!" the male cop said,
    And the white mom-cop shook up the can
    And did so with non-random, non-loving
    Hatred in her bored – I just want to go
    Home – heart. [45]

XLIX.

Over the shoulder of Washington,
    Ben. Franklin spied a half-sun
Carved into the back of America's chair.

He wondered if the effigy's light
　　Denoted a rising or setting sun;
And now we know the answer. [46]

L.

　　I read in the paper
　　　How the Rittenhouse verdict made
　　Arbery's mother "Anxious,"
　　　And the sight of it broke my heart.

　　　　　Why is it justice has to be
　　　　　So touch-and-go in our country?
　　　　　A cold-blooded murder by gun
　　　　　Wielded by any color hand –
　　　　　By crook or cop of any stripe;
　　　　　By self-appointed vigilante
　　　　　Of any political bent –
　　　　　Should receive the same court sentence.
　　　　　But, in our touch-and-go country,
　　　　　Cold-blooded murders get sorted
　　　　　By the wielder's color of hand;
　　　　　By their RAP sheet or police badge;
　　　　　By self-spouting vigilante
　　　　　Polarizing as excuse,
　　　　　So they don't get the same sentence.

　　I read in the paper
　　　How the Rittenhouse verdict made
　　Arbery's father "Upset,"
　　　And the sight of it broke my heart. [47]

LI.

Saint Rittenhouse,
The Right's new idol
Is less man than mouse.

A mortar smashed
By a pestles' shamelessness
Is a crucible waiting to be dashed.

And endless chicanery,
Glib as a teenage grin,
Their new idolatry.

LII.

Say Their Names II

Harum-Scarum backlash . . .

The powers that be
Lash out in ways reckless,
Irresponsibly set
To demonstrate to us
Who remains in control.
Just think how Colinford Mattis
And Urooj Rahman have fared,
Falsely arrested in Brooklyn
For 'disrespecting' a cop car
Already burned out by others,
These two privileged-but-Black lawyers
Were hauled in like common vandals.
After completing bail hearings
For the hyped-up, unprovable

Vandalism charges, they were
Released on bond amounts fitting
To such inconsequential 'crime.'
Then, after being home, a "judge" –
So-called, 'cause a Trump appointee –
Had them arrested *again,* and
Held over for trial without bail.
Say their names: Colinford Mattis
And Urooj Rahman still rotting
In a New York city jail today.

Harum-Scarum backlash . . .

Say the name of Terron J. Boone,
Cop-killed less than two weeks after
His brother Robert Fuller was
Hanged on a tree outside L.A. –
Coincidence L.A. sheriffs
Would just happen to go looking
For a lynching victim's family
To make further "example" of?
Of course, conveniently for them,
Their body cameras were turned off,
So it's their word of what happened
Against that of a dead man. Nice.

Harum-Scarum backlash . . .

Or Helter Skelter scheme –
Have boogie-woogie days
And cop nights of "slaughter"
Been happening all along,
To prove who's in control? [48]

LIII.

I won't lie –
  The sight of the triple conviction
Made me cry.

And here's why –
  Knowing Arbery's parents saw justice
Filled my eye.

¤{ }¤{ }¤{ }¤{ }¤
¤{ }¤{ }¤{ }¤
¤{ }¤{ }¤
¤{ }¤

Part Nine: dei ex machina
Environmental Collapse III

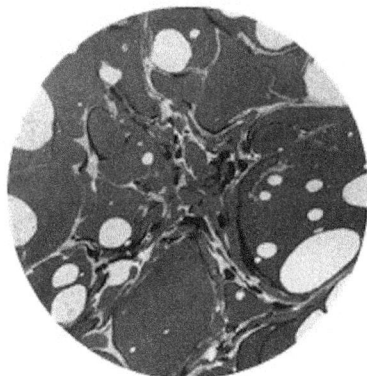

"America today stands poised
on a pinnacle of wealth and power,
yet we live in a land
of vanishing beauty,
of increasing ugliness,
of shrinking open space,
and of an over-all environment
that is diminished daily
by pollution, and noise, and blight."
—Stewart Udall,
1963 [49]

LIV.

Roundel

Such good news from New Delhi of a deadly smog—
News from London, the Themes is full of toxic sharks,
Though if you think we've reached some 'weird' highwater marks,
Know such 'Freaks of Nature' just start the catalog.

    'Cause it's not Nature's fault if Man's a demagogue,
    Pissing where we eat like dumb, fat-ass oligarchs;
    Such good news from New Delhi of a deadly smog—
    News from London, the Themes is full of toxic sharks.

We've made the world the mire through which we now must slog,
And no amount of finger-pointing or remarks
Can cool, or clean, or save forest fires from the sparks
When we're the tyrant, and Nature's the underdog.

    Such good news from New Delhi of a deadly smog—
    News from London, the Themes is full of toxic sharks! [50]

LV.

The New Normal

The New Norm, which we've yet to see,
    Was proposed fifty years ago
In a study by MIT.

Warmth, peace, comfort was all to go
        As a new Dark Age ushered in
Dog-eat-dog as we've yet to know.

With natural resources thin –
        Consumed and used up without care –
The World to Come will be a sin.

Acid and plagued will be the air;
        Poisoned and befouled the water;
Insects dead, famine everywhere;

Family son saved by selling daughter;
        No law except that of a gun;
No survival except through slaughter.

And though it might surprise to learn
        These scientific predictions –
Ignored, saying our homes will burn

Through a ruined Earth and human frictions –
        Have been around for fifty years,
Their numbers face no contradictions,

And in fact tell our nagging fears
        That 'this world can't go on' are true,
Though it's still falling on deaf ears.

2048 is the date –
        So mark your advanced calendar –
When your kids will live in a Failed State. [51]

LVI.

von **Das letzte Lied**

*(Nach dem Griechischen, aus dem
Zeitalter Philipps von Mazedonien)*

Fern ab am Horizont, auf Felsenrissen,
Liegt der gewitterschwarze Krieg getürmt.
Die Blitze zucken schon, die ungewissen,
Der Wandrer sucht das Laubdach, das ihn schirmt.
Und wie ein Strom, geschwellt von Regengüssen,
Aus seines Ufers Bette heulend stürmt,
Kommt das Verderben, mit entbundnen Wogen,
Auf alles, was besteht, herangezogen.
                    —Heinrich von Kleist,
                              1809

from **The Final Number**

*(After the Greek, from the
Age of Philip of Macedon)*

Off far horizons, in the cracks of the rock,
Dark and thunderous war begins its mounding.
The lightning twitches, and the weak feel the shock,
Running for cover, under trees abounding.
But like a torrent, the streams swell and unlock
Annihilation sweeping and surrounding,
Howling out of its banks as the doom sees fit
To wash over all trying to withstand it.
                    —Heinrich von Kleist,
                              1809 [52]

LVII.

What do you think can explain the mindset
Of dumping 25,000 barrels
Of DDT in the ocean, right off
The coast of L.A.'s most crowded beaches?

What explains the military mindset
Of forcing GIs to light bonfires
Of super-toxins with no protections
By order of King Bush I through his
Pentagon control in the early 90s?

What explains the hopelessness we now feel
From evil controlling the way we live –
From corrupt Gops and glib corporations –
To make a buck on human suffering,
Ruining every refuge the world has left
Because we're dumb brutes who shit where we eat. [53]

LVIII.

Poisoned Blood

Not only COVID
   is making humanity
Dumber, but manmade
   chemicals infect our brains.

         Human waste full of Prozac
         Pollutes every watershed
         Cities and towns tap into.
         Teflon is detected in every newborn.
         But if you think that is bad,
         It's the tip of the iceberg.

In the blood of the unborn
Flows plasticizers from food
Contamination on plates,
Forks, Single cups, and bottles.
The babies' blood also has
Flame retardants, pesticides,
High volume petroleum
Chemicals in abundance,
Pollution from artificial
Candle and aerosolized
Toxins used for fake fragrance,
And nearly 40 others
So top-secret in their
Military-Industrial
Complex uses their names are
Totally unknown to our
Healthcare service providers.
Here's what voting Gop gets you
And all your unborn children.

Not only tin foil
  is making humanity
Dumber, but manmade
  politics infect our blood. [54]

LIX.

Poisoned Air

China's pollution now
— in 2021 —
Is more massive than all
Emissions of the rest
Of the industrial
Countries' total combined.

Twenty years ago we
Could have been selling them
Clean solutions, but then
Lil Bushy Junior
Was in the pocket of
Big Oil, so no sale. [55]

LX.

THE EARTH AND YOUR CIRCADIAN RHYTHMS
vs.
THE MILITARY-INDUSTRIAL COMPLEX

We're so out of touch
    With Nature and Nature's God
We literally
    Don't know what time of day it is
'Cept by the clock's lying hands.
    Wake Up!

'The Man' barks we must
    Get up an hour early –
Telling us we're late! –
    Then keeps us one hour after work,
Snigg'ring how much time was 'Saved.'
    Wake Up!

We grope in the dark
    Ignoring our body's clock,
Feeling horrible,
    And *wonder* at the world's state
While we wither in our selves.
    Wake Up!

Rise up against this
    Daylight Pretend Time madness;
Refute your own lies
    Told by 'The Man' you like it,
Because you know, you HATE it!
    Wake Up! [56]

LXI.

In 2018, fossil fuel toxins
In the atmosphere killed some 8.7
Million people outright. So our not caring,
8.7 million times, is now Man's lot.
How easily we kill with our shoulder shrugs. [57]

LXII.

Who in the world today
    Thinks self-replicating robots
    Is something like a good idea?

And yet, now they exist,
    And 2021's the date
    Mankind crossed o'er this stupid line. [58]

¤{ }¤{ }¤{ }¤{ }¤
¤{ }¤{ }¤{ }¤
¤{ }¤{ }¤
¤{ }¤

Part Ten: Apophis
Finale, Mortar and Pestle

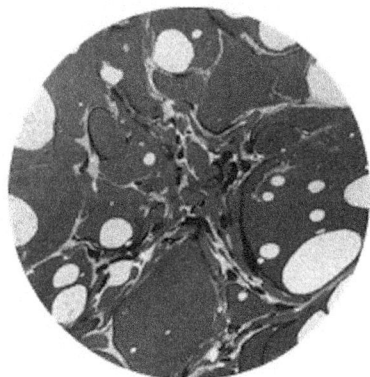

"The man who is swimming against the stream knows the strength of it."

—Woodrow Wilson,
circa 1916 [59]

LXIII.

Der höhere Frieden
von Heinrich von Kleist, 1792

Wenn sich auf des Krieges Donnerwagen,
    Menschen waffnen, auf der Zwietracht Ruf,
Menschen, die im Busen Herzen tragen,
    Herzen, die der Gott der Liebe schuf:

Denk ich, können sie doch mir nichts rauben,
    Nicht den Frieden, der sich selbst bewährt,
Nicht die Unschuld, nicht an Gott den Glauben,
    Der dem Hasse, wie dem Schrecken, wehrt.

Nicht des Ahorns dunkelm Schatten wehren,
    Daß er mich, im Weizenfeld, erquickt,
Und das Lied der Nachtigall nicht stören,
    Die den stillen Busen mir entzückt.

The Higher Peace
by Heinrich von Kleist, 1792

When arms the thunderbolts of war promote,
    Men to discord's call have oft obeyed,
Men with hearts they feel rising in their throat,
    Hearts that by the God of Love were made:

But they can nothing rob from me of note,
    Not the peace that proves itself most blessed,
Not innocence, which faith in God can quote
    To resist hate and terror with rest.

Therefore, fight not the deep shade, though remote,
    The maple tree in the wheat field's laid;
Where on the evening bird's song I may dote
    As in my silent bosom it's played. [60]

LXIV.

> *The wicked Gop's Tiananmen Square*
> *Did not take place, they swear.*
> *"January 6th?" they've come to snit,*
> *"**I've** never heard of it."*

With the elephant-brains foisting
the joke that the Capitol Insurrection
– led by them and their Big Lie –
was no big deal, they moved into
aping the Chinese Commie Party's
insistence the 1989 Revolution
was just some minor disturbance
in a public thoroughfare, somewhere . . . .

But now as the final days
of December 2021 come rolling along,
The Party in Hong Kong has
applied its evil power: arresting
truth-telling news agents;
tearing down monuments to
the victims of the tanks and others
forced to die instead of see China
liberated and free. The monuments
come down, the people are jailed,
tortured, perhaps to be executed
like so many were in June of 1989,
their families sent humiliating bills
for the 39-cents' worth of bullet
shot through their loved-one's
democracy-loving head.

This is a warning for how Gop
One-Party Rule will unfold in
the United States and don't doubt it.

For as my high school teacher
Mr. Dohle taught us back in the '80s,
– before Tiananmen didn't happen's Big Lie –
the extremists on the far left and right
like the Nazis and Stalinists
may be politically polar opposites,
but their techniques of oppression
meet up in exactly the same place.

So the Gop's new fiction that
January 6th, 2021, was "no big deal"
is the mirror copy of the Commie's
"never happened" there, on China's soil.
But then again, totalitarian parties
will be totalitarian parties,
so one cannot be too surprised
the Repubs have taken their horrible
'history argumentation' lessons
from Mao's lackeys, who still
cower behind the Forbidden City's
moldering walls in 2022. [61]

LXV.

Three hundred twenty-nine days.
    Three hundred twenty-nine days
Separate George Floyd's murder
    From twenty-six-year-old
Mario Gonzalez killed by
    Alameda cops. Cops on video
Shown kneeling on Mario's back until
    He was dead. Three of them.
Kneeling on one, handcuffed young man's
    Back until dead in the gravel.

The powers-that-be are still,
    To the day of writing this,
Refusing the release of
    His autopsy report;
Two hundred twenty-seven days
    His family's been robbed of the legal grounds
On which his killers could be indicted.
    Two hundred twenty-seven
Days justice has been subverted;
    Days which just go on piling up. [62]

LXVI.

What sadder lilac upon the threshold
Could bloom than to think Mario's family
Needed the crushing wherewithal to do
What George Floyd's family did and have their son's
Sacred, mortal remains autopsied by
A 3rd party coroner to ensure
The truth got out about his brutal killing;
To force the County of Alameda to tell the truth. [63]

LXVII.

"These victims of hallucinations
Not only revile that of which they
Have no knowledge, but are
Corrupted through the very things
They know by instincts, like brute
Animals, to be wholly untrue. [...]
They have abandoned themselves
To Balaam's error for money,
And like Korah, they perish
For their confrontational trickery. [...]

They eat your food without shame
While only looking out for themselves.

> *They are blown about on the winds*
> *As clouds that bring no rain.*
> *They are dead inside and*
> *Should be uprooted like the year-end*
> *Fruit trees that bear no wholesome yield.*
> *They are seasick waves producing*
> *Nothing but the be-fouled sputum*
> *Of foam to sicken others*
> *With their false deeds abroad.*
> *They are the thick fog of darkness*
> *Reserved solely to block out the celestial*
> *Light of shooting stars to enlighten.* [...]

Such men are grumblers and whiners,
Who live for their corporal pleasures
And utter only deceitful bombast. [...]
Remember, my belovèd man, these
Imposters living out their unholy groanings
– These groundings devoid of Christian Spirit –
Only revel in causing divisions among us."

—Epistle of Jude to his
partner, James,
brother of Jesus,
circa **60** A.D. [64]

LXVIII.

Elegy

When lilacs next in the doorway bloom,
My mourning weeds for a once-great society
Will need be donned; my tears, dried.

Lilacs bloom perennially, but no more
    Shall they be seen upon the threshold
Of our extinguished democracy.

Bloom and drooping star in the west
    Shall be the only signs left behind
As a thought for a country I loved.

LXIX.

We're soon to crest the summit of a hill
From whose vast terrain a darkness must grow –
A world where evil is the status quo
To smother America's last free will.
For now the Gops won't be happy until
They've made freedom our second Alamo
And set it ablaze as the final blow
On a Nation they've worked so long to kill.

      Yes, over that rise is a setting light,
      For their **2022** district-line
      Already assures Gop one-party rule.
      But, shall our Liberty bear arms and fight
      To try and make our setting sun re-shine?—
      Or is a second Civil War too cruel.

LXX.

Funny, but I never saw myself
    As a 'political' poet.

Instead, I assumed I'd always write
    Verse of a personal nature.

But now, a truer truth is clear to me:
    All politics are personal.

LXXI.

"IF—"
for an Immature Age

If you can damn a warm January day
    As part and parcel of a worldwide curse,
And not let the ignorance in you pipe up and say
    "Well, for winter, we could do a lot worse!";
If instead you long for the renewing snows
    Because they're more needed than weather mild,
Feeling proud how maturity in you grows,
    Then you will be an adult, my child.

If you can endure springtime showers and grin
    With a broadening sense of consciousness,
Ignoring your petty gripes when they begin
    And bless Nature's great advantageousness;
If instead you think of the wheat and flowers
    – Of bread for your offspring, with honey piled –
Standing humbled mid the thunderstorms' powers,
    Then you will be an adult, my child.

If you can bear the worst August and July
    With nary a complaint against the heat,
Knowing the insects need this time 'fore they die
    'Cause much of the world's covered in concrete;
If instead you're prosaic about the sweat
    And wipe your brow with a mind reconciled,
Accepting that it's better to give than get,
    Then you will be an adult, my child.

If you can watch an autumn sunset go down
    And not think what you glimpse is beautiful
Due to tons of sulphur-dioxide brown
    Never letting you see the sun in full;
If instead you lament wicked pollution
    Covering the Earth as it's now defiled
And feel renewed to finding a solution,
    Then you will be an adult, my child!

LXXII.

How harshly those in the future
Will look back on us, thinking,
"How easy they had it compared to us."
But then again, remember, the world
They're forced to live in
Is wholly our doing.

What they will have to do to survive,
We cannot even begin to imagine
Because we think we have it so bad;
Because we let division and strife
Drill in our heads for the oil of ignorance;
Because we won't man up and love one another.

LXXIII.

How long ago it feels our Nation had
A leader willing to make the world safe
For democracy where tyrants forbad
Any Liberties that might result in strafe.
And how long ago now it seems we heard
A President list every person's right

To Freedom from Want, from a Censor's Word,
From an Oppressor's Hand, and Fear's dark Strife.
Replaced are these with one Party's horsemen;
The Gop's Conquest, War, Starvation and Death,
Running hot in apostate adrenaline
To pronounce our way of life shibboleth.
    Look for no salvation from the Rule of Law,
    Whose back they keep riding to overawe. [65]

LXXIV.

Too Little; Too Late

i.
What We Do Today

Twenty years ago was the time to save
    Our Democracy from foreign,
Yellow newscasting, which made the public
    Get lost in an Aussie warren.
Media Reform of FDR's type
    – To restore the Fair and Balanced –
Is what America needed the most . . .
    But the Dems acted unconvinced.

Thus, in the absence of leadership, see
    Mobs of the coerced and kowtowed
Attacking those who would help their children
    Think thoughts beyond the merely loud.
Two decades back, something could have been done
    To stop Trump's January goons
Breaking into Congress with rope nooses,
    Acting as told by rich tycoons.

ii.
The Environmental Economy

Twenty years ago, our "leaders" – who were
    All cash-and-carry property
Of lobbyists – killed California law
    For Detroit's Irrelevant Three.
Emission-neutral transport set in stone,
    And signed by a Gop governor,
Forced companies to hybrid engines
    And sell them, causing quite a stir.

Toyota brought the Prius to market
    Because the public wanted it;
GM built the electric EV1
    To rule over the new-car gambit.
But instead of selling us GM cars,
    They paid to hurt the citizens,
Denying the world the clean vehicle
    GM could have sold in the billions.

iii.
Myth-Making Politics

So, here we are, their lies so outrageous,
    Shed upon a people so dumb,
Gop one-party tyranny is at hand:
    A gun-mad society come
Where the angst is NRA-approved for
    Mass murder; where this gun cancer
Militarized all community-based
    Policing like it was an answer.

Now when the allegèd 'good guys' cry out
    "Let's roll!", they do it from the top

Of Army Humvees with machine gun locked,
    Manned by some antsy traffic cop:
Two decades of this unlicensed slaughter,
    By shit-pancing a dim public
Has othered those of America's own
    And brought to heel this Republic.

iv.
"Forgive me" –
Social Justice

2021, a Detroit car firm
    Announced they'd go all electric . . .
Starting at some vague date in the future . . .
    But it's just another gimmick.
Everything now is 20 years too late –
    Too late to save us from a fall,
And our selfish age must come to an end,
    For too little's too late overall.

Yet humans, we like our Ray of Hope talk,
    Spreading it on thick as manure,
But telling shit from shinola's a prob
    With optimism's base allure.
Hope-talk – thinking "they'll fix it down the line" –
    Got us into this quagmire.
No one's coming to pull us from the muck,
    And my tepid words won't inspire. [66]

¤{ }¤{ }¤{ }¤{ }¤
¤{ }¤{ }¤{ }¤
¤{ }¤{ }¤
¤{ }¤

A last plea from the
last day of the year

I think of him there,
kicked out of the
Presidential Bed
by the late-come,
undocumented, First Lady.

Alone, exiled from the
third floor, from 'wife' and child,
he bedded in a second floor room
– all top secret, of course –
and no doubt he encountered
The White House's most
famous, permanent resident.

Queens and Prime Ministers
have seen him; spoken to him.
Housemaids and footmen know
of his regular steps in the night,
the pacing with restlessness
for a job undone: the healing
of wounds; the righting of
racial wrongs; forgiveness.

So, what in the juvenile mind
of Donald Trump could he think
when Lincoln's ghost appeared to him?
The Soul of our Nation, slaughtered
on the Union Altar of absolution,
materialized to deliver
a valuable lesson
to a loser-man like Trump?

I think of him there,
Singled out, exiled, on one of
his self-pitying evenings,
Totally alone in the world,
sweating and nauseous,
coked up yet again in his despair,
confronted by true greatness.
And what more damning words
could America's Shade
say to that quivering failure
of a human existence?

No more than what the national crisis
in the offing could have told him:
what the little boy in Donald Trump
has known all along, in every
situation where the adults are:
"You do not belong here!
You are unworthy of title,
Of respect, of even freedom.
You, sir, must go your way
And trouble a nation of troubles
No more. You let the Stars and Bars
Be raised over the People's Congress,
For which there is no penance.
Be gone from this House.
Be gone from our cognizance.
Be outcast from Our memories
For ever and aye!" [67]

Notes and Sources

The updatable nature of the internet means some material documented here may have been moved or deleted. If so, copy the name of the content and content—creator and search online. Alternates will most likely be very easy to find.

ACB

[1] Notes for Epigraph: *January 6, 2021*
"A crime that robs one of sleep in the night"

A stark list of collaborators from inside the Capitol. See Tammy Marie Rose's *Peter Navarro Implicates Ted Cruz, Paul Gosar and 100 Other Congressmen in Planned Coup to Overthrow the 2020 Election* posted in vozwire.com

https://vozwire.com/peter-navarro-implicates-ted-cruz-paul-gosar-and-100-other-congressmen-in-planned-coup-to-overthrow-the-2020-election/?fbclid=IwAR0ufCFZJWThaHwKJ4hsX7j1_RZ8ICerQPyPSyMTcEuw4Djy1plWpoDT4lo

– And for the Stars and Bars wavers from within the federal government in on the coup, see Ed Pilkington's January 5th, 2022, article *More Than 1,000 U.S. Public Figures Aided Trump's Efforts to Overthrow Election* posted on theguardian.com

https://www.theguardian.com/us-news/2022/jan/05/trump-capitol-attack-democracy-election-insurrection-index

– Also see Martin Pengelly's January 2nd, 2022, article – mere days from the 1st anniversary of the Capitol Insurrection – *Capitol Attack: Cheney says Republicans must choose between Trump and Truth: Republican member of the House Committee investigating the events of [January 6th] issues stark warning to her party. 'We can either be loyal to Trump, or the Constitution – but not both!'* posted on theguardian.com

https://www.theguardian.com/us-news/2022/jan/02/capitol-attack-liz-cheney-republicans-choose-trump-or-truth

[2] Notes for the Part One Epigraph:
"God offers to every mind its choice" Ralph Waldo Emerson *Intellect,* reprinted in *Pegs to Hang Ideas on; a Book of Quotations* [Marjorie Weiser, Editor] (New York 1973), p. 213

https://archive.org/details/pegstohangideaso0000weis/page/212/mode/2up

[3] Note for Verse No. 1 (I):
"Remember January 6th"

Remember the Gops did it; did it all. See Andrea González-Ramírez's January 6th, 2021, article *A List of Everyone Complicit in This Coup Attempt: For Months, Trump Has Lied About the 2020 Election and Enabled This Violence* posted on gen.medium.com

https://gen.medium.com/a-list-of-everyone-complicit-in-this-coup-attempt-1fb54331f76b

[4] Notes for Verse No. 2 (II):
"Forgive and forget"

Fuck them. See Letters to the Editor: May 28th, 2021, *Republicans Want Us to Forget Jan. 6, Just Like We Did the Tulsa Massacre* posted on latimes.com

https://www.latimes.com/opinion/story/2021-05-28/republicans-want-us-to-forget-jan-6

[5] Notes for Verse No. 3 (III):
"What Bozos – those who ranked The Dumpster"

*Follow history too closely on its heels, and be prepared to get kicked in the teeth.** Such are they who ranked the Dumpster-fire the 4th worst president in history *BEFORE* January 6th. See Alison Durkee's January 19th, 2021, article *Polls: Half of Americans View Trump Presidency as a Failure* posted on forbes.com

https://www.forbes.com/sites/alisondurk
ee/2021/01/19/polls-half-of-americans-
view-trump-presidency-as-a-
failure/?sh=716822ac68e0

* The complete, accurate quote comes from no less an historical figure than Walter Raleigh: "Whosoever, in writing a modern history, shall follow truth too near the heels, it may haply strike out his teeth." (1614)

– And see Lance Lambert's January 11th, 2021, article *Trump to Leave Office with the Worst Jobs Record Since Herbert Hoover* posted on fortune.com

https://fortune.com/2021/01/11/us-economy-jobs-numbers-trump-compared-past-presidents-worst-record-since-hoover/

– Also see Dan Barry's November 26th, 2021, article *'Loser': How a Lifelong Fear Bookended Trump's Presidency* posted on nytimes.com

https://www.nytimes.com/2020/11/26/us/politics/trump-election-loss.html

– Also see Lauren Victoria Burke's January 4th, 2021, article *Donald Trump Spent Almost a Year Playing Golf During Presidency* posted on seatlemedium.com

https://seattlemedium.com/donald-trump-spent-almost-a-year-playing-golf-during-presidency/

[6] Notes for Verse No. 5 (V): Sonnet
"If there's a hope in this world, it might come"

It was inevitable their own kids, raised on good American values, would reject the modern Gop shitshow. See David Li / Rima Abdelkader's January 26th, 2021, article *People are Turning in Family Members, Ex-Romantic Partners They Recognize in Capitol Riot Video: Children, Siblings and Spouses Were Horrified Watching the Insurrection – Especially When They Spotted People They Knew in the Crowd* posted on nbcnews.com

https://www.nbcnews.com/news/us-
news/people-are-turning-family-
members-ex-romantic-partners-they-
recognize-n1254597

– And see Kristen Wong's February 4th, 2021, article *What Happens to the Teens Who Turned in Their Parents for Participating in the Capitol Riot?* posted on verygoodlight.com

https://verygoodlight.com/2021/02/04/te
ens-turned-in-parents-capitol-
insurrection

– Also see Kari Paul's January 17th, 2021, article *'I Had No Qualms': The People Turning in Loved Ones for the Capitol Attack: The Majority of More Than 140,000 Tips Sent to the FBI About the Attack Have Come from Friends and Family of Those Involved* posted on theguardian.com

https://www.theguardian.com/us-news/2021/jan/17/capitol-attack-reporting-family-internet-sleuths-qanon

– Also see Ronnie Koenig's August 23rd, 2020, article *Kelleyanne Conway's Daughter Claudia, 15, Says She's Seeking Emancipation: The 15-Year-Old Has Been Outspoken on Social Media Against her Parents' Political Views* posted on nbcchicago.com

https://www.nbcchicago.com/news/politics/kellyanne-conways-daughter-claudia-15-says-shes-seeking-emancipation/2326971/

– Also see Travis Gettys' December 30th, 2021, article *Ted Cruz's Daughter Knocks Him on TikTok: "I Really*

Disagree with Most of His Views posted on salon.com

https://www.salon.com/2021/12/30/ted-cruzs-daughter-knocks-him-on-tiktok-i-really-disagree-with-most-of-his-views_partner/

[7] Notes for Verse No. 6 (VI): Ballade
"Septimius Severus lives in my song"

The root of gun-mad 'Merican brain-rot? See Sean Illing's January 5th, 2022, article *The Gop's Masculinity Panic: David French on the Cult of Toughness on the Trumpist Right* posted on vox.com

https://www.vox.com/vox-conversations-podcast/22834353/vox-conversations-david-french-republican-party-trump-masculinity

[8] Note for the Part Two Epigraph:
"The mind of the bigot is like the pupil of the eye" Oliver Wendell Holmes, Junior *The Harper Book of Quotations* [Robert Fitzhenry, Editor] (New York 1993), p. 369

https://archive.org/details/fitzhenrywhite si0000unse_p9g3/page/368/mode/2up

[9] Note for Verse No. 9 (IX):
"John Sullivan, Utah progressive"

For the Black man's handling being initially more severe than fellow January 6th white participants, see Josh Gerstein's January 14th, 2021, article *Liberal Utah Activist Charged with Joining Capitol Riot* posted on politico.com

https://www.politico.com/news/2021/01/
14/liberal-activist-charged-capitol-riot-
459553

[10] Note for Verse No. 10 (X):
"Segregation dead in Louisiana?"
Deputy Sheriff's burial. See The Associated Press' January 29th, 2021, article *Black Deputy Denied Burial in Louisiana Cemetery Due to his Race* re-posted on cbsnews.com

https://www.cbsnews.com/news/darrell-
semien-black-deputy-denied-burial-
louisiana-cemetery-race/

[11] Note for Verse No. 12 (XII):
"What in our 'blessèd' world"

Saint Charles, Missouri, teachers. See Gina Spocchia's March 5th, 2021, article *Missouri Teachers Under Fire for Photograph Spelling Out Racial Slur in Giant Letters: 'There Are No Consequences for People's Actions, and it's Demoralising [sic],' Says Parent* posted on independent.co.uk

https://www.independent.co.uk/news/wo
rld/americas/missouri-teachers-racist-
photo-scrabble-b1812961.html

[12] Note for the Part Three Epigraph:
"When I hear of the destruction of a species" Theodore Roosevelt, private letter to Frank M. Chapman, reprinted in *Pegs to Hang Ideas on; a Book of Quotations* [Marjorie Weiser, Editor] (New York 1973), p. 247

https://archive.org/details/pegstohangide
aso0000weis/page/246/mode/2up

[13] Note for Verse No. 13 (XIII):
"Three Triolets on a Theme"

The world is literally on fire now, all year long. See Lisa Shumaker / Andrea Januta's December 13th, 2021, article *From Wildfires to Floods, Climate Change*

Worsens Extreme Weather Across Globe posted on insurancejournal.com

https://www.insurancejournal.com/news/
international/2021/12/13/645400.htm

[14] Notes for Verse No. 14 (XIV):
"Twenty-three, the species declared extinct"

Reality-based reality catches up listing exterminated species due to manmade conditions. See Catrin Einhorn's September 28th, 2021, article *Protected Too Late: U.S. Officials Report More Than 20 Extinctions* posted on nytimes.com

https://www.nytimes.com/2021/09/28/cli
mate/endangered-animals-extinct.html

– And CBS / Associated Press' September 29th, 2021, article *Ivory-Billed Woodpecker, 22 Other Species Declared Extinct by U.S. Government* posted on cbsnews.com

https://www.cbsnews.com/news/ivory-billed-woodpecker-23-species-declared-extinct-us/

[15] Notes for Verse No. 15 (XV): Kyrielle
"The young are without hope the Earth"

Reality-based reality in the young's view of Baby Boomers' crass disregard for the survival of the human species. See Rob Picheta's October 25th, 2021, article *CO2 Levels in the Atmosphere Reach a 3 Million-Year High, Putting the World 'Way Off Track'* posted on cnn.com

https://www.cnn.com/2021/10/25/world/
emissions-climate-greenhouse-gas-
bulletin-wmo-intl/index.html

– And Sharon Pruitt-Young's September 11th, 2021, article *Climate Change is Making Natural Disasters Worse – Along with Our Mental Health* posted on npr.org

https://www.npr.org/2021/09/11/103524
1392/climate-change-disasters-mental-
health-anxiety-eco-grief

– Also see Steffan Messenger's June 24th, 2021, article *Climate Change Anxiety: Young People 'Feel Hopeless'* posted on bbc.com

https://www.bbc.com/news/uk-wales-57555760

[16] Note for Verse No. 17 (XVII):
"Why should I be shocked?—"

The stripping of Brazil. See Liz Kimbrough's October 6th, 2021, article *Brazil Leads Amazon in Forest Loss This Year* posted on news.mongabay.com

https://news.mongabay.com/2021/10/brazil-leads-amazon-in-forest-loss-this-year-indigenous-territories-and-parks-hold-out/

– And see the European Space Agency's October 6th, 2021, article *Forest Degradation Primary Driver of Carbon Loss in the Brazilian Amazon* posted on esa.int

https://www.esa.int/Applications/Observing_the_Earth/Space_for_our_climate/Forest_degradation_primary_driver_of_carbon_loss_in_the_Brazilian_Amazon

https://www.esa.int/var/esa/storage/images/esa_multimedia/images/2021/06/forest_loss_in_the_amazon_basin/23343124-4-eng-GB/Forest_loss_in_the_Amazon_basin_article.gif

Compare the satellite view of Brazil in 2021 (above) with this eoportal.org satellite image taken in 2000

https://directory.eoportal.org/image/imag
e_gallery?uuid=66356af9-0f6c-44ea-
a613-
f53768c42f09&groupId=163813&t=1338
223710347

The following businessinsider.com map pinpoints the nearly 40,000 out-of-control forest fires in South America for the summer of 2019 alone, although hundreds of thousands of additional acres have burned since then

https://i.insider.com/5d5ef09badbcf8373
954f386?width=700&format=jpeg&auto=
webp

– And Aylin Woodward's August 23rd, 2019, article *Brazil Has Seen 100,000 Fire Alerts in 10 Days, But it's not Just the Amazon – One Map Shows How Much of*

South America is Burning posted on businessinsider.com

https://www.businessinsider.com/map-
south-america-on-fire-amazon-2019-8

[17] Notes for Verse No. 18 (XVIII):
"Biomass, Biomass, you can't compete"

Manmade junk. See Drew Kann's December 9th, 2020,
article *Human-Made Materials May Now Outweigh All Living
Things on Earth* posted on cnn.com

https://www.cnn.com/2020/12/09/world/
human-made-mass-exceeds-biomass-
report-2020/index.html

– And Patrick Galey's December 9th, 2020, article *Manmade Mass Now Outweighs Life on Earth* posted on phys.org

https://phys.org/news/2020-12-manmade-mass-outweighs-life-earth.html

[18] Notes for Verse No. 19 (XIX): Sonnet "How many have been the poems written"

Rains in Greenland. See Joe Hernandez's August 20th, 2021, article *Rain Fell on the Peak of Greenland's Ice Sheet for the First Time in Recorded History* posted on npr.org

https://www.npr.org/2021/08/20/1029633740/rain-fall-peak-of-greenland-ice-sheet-first-climate-change

– And Rachel Ramirez's August 19th, 2021, article *Rain Fell at the Normally Snowy Summit of Greenland for First Time on Record* posted on cnn.com

https://www.cnn.com/2021/08/19/weath
er/greenland-summit-rain-climate-
change/index.html

[19] Note for the Part Four Epigraph:
"By gnawing through a dyke" Edmund Burke *The Harper Book of Quotations* [Robert Fitzhenry, Editor] (New York 1993), p. 388

https://archive.org/details/fitzhenrywhite
si0000unse_p9g3/page/388/mode/2up

[20] Note for Verse No. 20 (XX):
"The ultimate symbol of elitism"

A Trump shooting spree is *A-OKAY* with the GOP [Grand Ole Partisans]. See Ali Vitali's January 23rd, 2016, article *Trump Says He Could 'Shoot Somebody' and Still Maintain Support: "I Could Stand in the Middle of Fifth Avenue and Shoot Somebody – Okay – And I Wouldn't Lose Any Voters – Okay?"* posted on nbcnews.com

https://www.nbcnews.com/politics/2016-election/trump-says-he-could-shoot-somebody-still-maintain-support-n502911

[21] Note for Verse No. 23 (XXIII): Sestina
"This then is the Gop's idea of kinder"

Skeletor is at it again. See Jordain Carney's June 1st, 2021, article *McConnell Signals Concern Over Changes to Qualified Immunity in Police Reform* posted on thehill.com

https://thehill.com/homenews/senate/55
6321-mcconnell-signals-concern-on-
changes-to-qualified-immunity

[22] Note for Verse No. 24 (XXIV):
"What could be more *hateful* in this country"
Jim Crow saves Gop ass over and over. See Ed Kilgore's
February 6th, 2021, article *What the Filibuster Has Cost
America* posted on nymag.com

https://nymag.com/intelligencer/2021/02/
how-much-has-the-filibuster-cost-
america.html

[23] Note for the Part Five Epigraph:
"The [African American] says, 'Now.'" Lyndon Baines
Johnson Memorial Day speech at Gettysburg National
Cemetery, reprinted in *Pegs to Hang Ideas on; a Book of*

Quotations [Marjorie Weiser, Editor] (New York 1973), p. 106

https://archive.org/details/pegstohangide
aso0000weis/page/106/mode/2up

[24] Notes for Verse No. 27 (XXVII):
"Let's play a game, shall we?"

Little girl in chains. See Jenn Selva's October 21st, 2021, article *A Black Girl Was Arrested at School in Hawaii Over a Drawing that Upset a Parent* posted on cnn.com

https://www.cnn.com/2021/10/20/us/haw
aii-black-girl-arrested-drawing-
aclu/index.html

From sleep to death in a matter of seconds. See Pehal News Team's October 21st, 2021, article *He Was Asleep in his Car. Police Woke Him Up and Created a Reason to Kill Him* posted on pehalnews.in

https://www.pehalnews.in/he-was-asleep-in-his-car-police-woke-him-up-and-created-a-reason-to-kill-him/1175448/

[25] Notes for Verse No. 29 (XXIX):
"No happy endings"

No justice for Luke's killing. See Sarah Gelsomino's October 21st, 2021, article *He Was Asleep in his Car. Police Woke Him Up and Created a Reason to Kill Him: An Officer Attacked Luke Stewart As He Was Sleeping in his Car and then Killed Him. Qualified Immunity Prevents Luke's Family From Receiving Justice* posted on usatoday.com

https://www.usatoday.com/story/opinion/
2021/10/21/qualified-immunity-police-
killed-luke-stewart/5711758001/

– And Alyssa Guzman's October 22nd, 2021, article *Lawyer Details Agony for Family of Black Man Killed by Ohio Cops After They Woke Him Sleeping in His Car, Yanked Him Out, Beat Him, Then Shot Him Five Times in 2017: Two Officers Involved Still Haven't Been Brought to Justice* posted on dailymail.co.uk

https://www.dailymail.co.uk/news/article-
10120549/Lawyer-details-agony-family-
black-man-killed-Ohio-cops-2017.html

[26] Notes for Verse No. 30 (XXX):
"Guess the color of Kyle Rittenhouse's judge"

No wounded need apply for justice. See Erik Ortiz's October 27th, 2021, article *Rittenhouse Judge in Spotlight After Disallowing Word 'Victims' in Courtroom* posted on nbcnews.com

https://www.nbcnews.com/news/us-news/rittenhouse-judge-spotlight-after-disallowing-word-victims-courtroom-n1282559

Arbery's jury. See Joe Hernandez's November 5th, 2021, article *How the Jury in the Ahmaud Arbery Case Ended up Nearly All White – And Why It Matters* posted on npr.org

https://www.npr.org/2021/11/05/105243 5205/ahmaud-arbery-jury

‒ And Devon Sayers / Alta Spells / Christina Maxouris' November 12th, 2021, article *Judge Says 'There Appears to be Intentional Discrimination' in Arbery Jury Selection, but Allows Trail to Move Forward with 1 Black Juror* posted on cnn.com

https://www.cnn.com/2021/11/03/us/ah maud-arbery-jury-what-we-know/index.html

‒ Also see CBS / The Associated Press' November 25th, 2021, article *Former Georgia Attorney Booked on Charges of Obstructing Ahmaud Arbery Case* posted on cbsnews.com

https://www.cbsnews.com/news/jackie-johnson-ahmaud-arbery-prosecutor-charged-obstruction/

[27] Notes for Verse No. 31 (XXXI):
"Audre Lorde knows what I mean"

Lorde's poem "Power"

https://www.poetryfoundation.org/poems
/53918/power-56d233adafeb3

Lorde's poem "Outlines" I

https://books.google.com/books?id=c5V
rCwAAQBAJ&pg=PT314&lpg=PT314&d
q=audre+lorde+%22what+hue+lies+in+t
he+slit%22&source=bl&ots=SMRDEkL8
ql&sig=ACfU3U1tzkbMMvXPFV_nflg6S
WGOEYH-
Ww&hl=en&sa=X&ved=2ahUKEwiU57L
u-
Yv0AhV8STABHfq_DWsQ6AF6BAgME
AM#v=onepage&q&f=false

[28] Notes for Verse No. 32 (XXXII): Tanka
"The day rises cold"

Image of ripening nandina berries:

https://upload.wikimedia.org/wikipedia/c
ommons/thumb/e/e4/Nandina_domestic
a_berries-
5142~2016_01_03.JPG/1280px-
Nandina_domestica_berries-
5142~2016_01_03.JPG

[29] Note for the Part Six Epigraph:
"It is not always *the other person* who pollutes" John F.
Kennedy remarks delivered to the Institute for Conservation,
reprinted in *Pegs to Hang Ideas on; a Book of Quotations*
[Marjorie Weiser, Editor] (New York 1973), p. 247

https://archive.org/details/pegstohangide
aso0000weis/page/246/mode/2up

[30] Notes for Verse No. 33 (XXXIII):
"Morning's First Glimpse, Sept. 6th, 2021"

Crazy, record-wrecking weather. See Jacob Feuerstein's
December 27th, 2021, article *Historic U.S. Weather Events
in 2021, by the Numbers* posted on washingtonpost.com

https://www.washingtonpost.com/weath
er/2021/12/27/2021-weather-records/

[31] Notes for Verse No. 34 (XXXIV):
"The kitchen table is clean"

Relentless forest- and wild fires. See Gabrielle Canon's December 25th, 2021, article *What the Numbers Tells* [sic] *Us About a Catastrophic Year of Wildfires* posted on theguardian.com

https://www.theguardian.com/us-news/2021/dec/25/what-the-numbers-tells-us-about-a-catastrophic-year-of-wildfires

[32] Notes for Verse No. 35 (XXXV):
"How out of touch are we"

Subway car drownings. See Sinéad Baker's July 22nd, 2021, article *Desperate Texts Show People Pleading for Help Inside Flooded Subway Trains in China, Where 12 People Drowned* posted on insider.com

https://www.insider.com/desperate-texts-stuck-china-zhengzhou-flooded-subway-12-died-2021-7

Drownings in New York. See Christopher Maag's September 2nd, 2021, article *Ida: New York City Reels from Surprise Flooding and Drowning Deaths* posted on northjersey.com

https://www.northjersey.com/story/news/columnists/christopher-maag/2021/09/02/hurricane-ida-nyc-deaths-officials-blame-climate-change/5698825001/

[33] Notes for Verse No. 36 (XXXVI):
"Glasgow 2021 – Climate Summit"

Summit overview. See Dan Charles' November 1st, 2021, article *The COP26 Summit to Fight Climate Change Has Started: Here's What to Expect* posted on npr.org

https://www.npr.org/2021/10/25/104761
7334/cop26-summit-climate-change-un-
glasgow

Queenly opt-out. See Rob Evans / David Pegg's July 28th, 2021, article *Queen Secretly Lobbied Scottish Ministers for Climate Law Exemption: Monarch Used Secretive Procedure to be Only Person in Country Not Bound by a Green Energy Rule* posted on theguardian.com

https://www.theguardian.com/uk-news/2021/jul/28/queen-secretly-lobbied-scottish-ministers-climate-law-exemption

– Makes her a 'comrade' with KGB Putin and his opt-out power as well. See Jennifer Peltz's December 13th, 2021, article *Russia Vetoes UN Resolution Linking Climate Change, Security* re-posted on abcnews.go.com

https://abcnews.go.com/US/wireStory/russia-vetoes-resolution-linking-climate-change-security-81725579

[34] Notes for Verse No. 37 (XXXVII):
"It was nearly 20 years ago now"

Lil Bushy Jr.'s oyle slur. See David Sandalow's February 3rd, 2006, article *President Bush and Oil Addiction* posted on brookings.edu

https://www.brookings.edu/opinions/pres
ident-bush-and-oil-addiction/

Now there are *TWO* holes in the ozone. See Jeremy Deaton's October 9th, 2021, article *Research Sheds Light on How Unusual North Pole Ozone Hole Formed Last Year* posted on washingtonpost.com

https://www.washingtonpost.com/weath
er/2021/10/09/north-pole-ozone-hole-
studies/

Japan's current whale slaughter. See a number of articles on the Whale and Dolphin Conservation USA's webpage *Whaling in Japan* – where that nation's 2021 killing season is quoted as 171 minke whales, 187 Bryde whales, and 25 sei whales, a majority of which were pregnant females – posted on whales.org

https://us.whales.org/our-4-goals/stop-whaling/whaling-in-japan/

Norway's 2021 whale cull. See The Animal Welfare Institute's February 23rd, 2021, press release *Norway Continues Whale Slaughter with 2021 Hunting Quota* – which is quoted as 1,278 minke whales – posted on awionline.org

https://awionline.org/press-releases/norway-continues-whale-slaughter-2021-hunting-quota

– Also see [14] Note for Verse No. 17 (XVII): "Why should I be shocked?—" for the Amazon forest devastation, which is now past the point of recovery

[35] Notes for Verse No. 38 (XXXVIII):
"For the ecological year"

More than a foot of snow for Hawaii. See Meredith Deliso's December 3rd, 2021, article *Blizzard Warnings Issued for Hawaii with at Least 12 Inches of Snow Forecast: Wind Gusts Over 100 mph Are Also Anticipated on the Big Island* posted abcnews.go.com

https://abcnews.go.com/US/blizzard-warning-issued-hawaii-12-inches-snow-forecast/story?id=81542659

[36] Notes for Verse No. 39 (XXXIX): Lai
"Insect collapse, it's a *fait accompli*"

Insect collapse. See Dave Goulson's July 25th, 2021, article *The Insect Apocalypse, 'Our World Will Grind to a Halt Without Them': Insects Have Declined by 75% in the Past 50 Years* posted on theguardian.com

https://www.theguardian.com/environment/2021/jul/25/the-insect-apocalypse-our-world-will-grind-to-a-halt-without-them

The great fish kill-off. See Craig Raleigh's March 3rd, 2021, article *A Third of All Freshwater Fish Face Extinction, According to New Research* posted on wideopenspaces.com

https://www.wideopenspaces.com/third-of-all-freshwater-fish-face-extinction/

[37] Note for the Part Seven Epigraph:
"The doctrine of the Strong shall Dominate" Franklin Delano Roosevelt's live radio address to the world on Christmas Eve 1943, in the middle of the Second World

War. The audio is available here, beginning at minute 44:38

https://youtu.be/BT3DyAu9Rqc

[38] Notes for Verse No. 40 (XL): Five Cinquains
"A BRIDGE TO THE 22ND CENTURY"

Clinton's Second Inaugural Address. See the complete text on bartleby.com

https://www.bartleby.com/124/pres65.html

Summary of the dead heroes from Jan. 6th. See Olivia Rubin / Alexander Mallin / Will Steakin's *By the Numbers: How the Jan. 6 Investigation is Shaping Up 1 Year Later* posted on abcnews.go.com

https://abcnews.go.com/US/numbers-jan-investigation-shaping-year/story?id=82057743

[39] Notes for Verse No. 41 (XLI):
"One-Party rule is what"

For a summary of Karl Rove's Gop gameplan of one-Party rule for the United States, see Craig Unger's August 7th, 2012, article *Boss Rove* posted on vanityfair.com

https://www.vanityfair.com/news/politics/2012/09/karl-rove-gop-craig-unger

[40] Notes for Verse No. 42 (XLII): Kyrielle
"Now each Gop-controlled state boldly employs"

The Dumpster tells supporters to vote for him more than once. See Lauren Egan's September 3rd, 2020, article *Trump Doubles Down on Encouraging Supporters to Vote Twice, Which is Illegal* posted on nbcnews.com

https://www.nbcnews.com/politics/2020-
election/trump-doubles-down-
encouraging-supporters-vote-twice-
which-illegal-n1239265

Arrests of Dump-head voters voting more than once. See The Associated Press' December 14th, 2021, article *Voters in Florida Retirement Community The Villages Charged with Multiple Votes in 2020 Election,* reposted on marketmatch.com

https://www.marketwatch.com/story/vote
rs-in-florida-retirement-community-the-
villages-charged-with-casting-multiple-
votes-in-2020-election-01639523181

Evil Gop battleplans to steal even more national elections. See David Daley's January 10th, 2022, article *Seven Ways Republicans Are Already Undermining the 2024 Election* posted on the guardian.com

https://www.theguardian.com/commenti
sfree/2022/jan/10/republicans-election-
democracy-seven-ways-trump

‒ And Fredreka Schouten's January 9th, 2022, article *Pro-Trump Republicans Try to Rewrite State Election Laws as a Voting Rights Showdown Looms in Congress* posted on cnn.com

https://www.cnn.com/2022/01/09/politics
/gop-election-voting-rights-battleground-
states/index.html

Hervis Rogers persecution. See Gino Nuzzolillo's July 15th, 2021, article *Arrested for Voting? Hervis Rogers and the Case Against Disappearing our Voters* posted on southerncoalition.org

https://southerncoalition.org/op-ed-
arrested-for-voting-hervis-rogers-and-
the-case-against-disappearing-our-
voters/

– And Ed Lavandera / Chris Boyette / Veronica Stracqualursi's July 11th, 2021, article *Texas Man Who Waited 'Over Six Hours' last Super Tuesday to Vote now Faces Illegal Voting Charges* posted on cnn.com

https://www.cnn.com/2021/07/11/politi
cs/hervis-rogers-texas-voting-
charge/index.html

[41] Notes for Verse No. 45 (XLV):
"January 20th, 2021"

Inaugural benediction's slur on Gay people. See The Biden Inaugural Committee's January 20th, 2021, video *Rev. Doctor Beaman Gives the Inauguration Benediction* posted on youtube.com

https://www.youtube.com/watch?v=v-
UF5_ntFBE

[42] Notes for Verse No. 46 (XLVI):
"It's something any seven-year-old in this country"

The fall of Saigon / the fall of Kabul. See Madalene Xuan-Trang Mielke's November 4th, 2021, article *My Family Fled Vietnam when I was 13: I See My Story in Every Afghan Trying to Escape* posted on msnbc.com

https://www.msnbc.com/know-your-value/my-family-fled-vietnam-when-i-was-3-i-see-n1283201

Willie-Horton-lie politics. See Mehdi Hasan's December 1st, 2018, article *The Ignored Legacy of George H. W. Bush: War Crimes, Racism, and Obstruction of Justice* posted on theintercept.com

https://theintercept.com/2018/12/01/the-ignored-legacy-of-george-h-w-bush-war-crimes-racism-and-obstruction-of-justice/

The slaughter of innocents by King Herod-Bush I in Panama City. Read survivors' firsthand accounts in John Otis' December 20th, 1989, article *U.S. Attack Devastates Poor Panama City Neighborhood* posted on upi.com

https://www.upi.com/Archives/1989/12/2 0/US-attack-devastates-poor-Panama-City-neighborhood/9411511037198/

The Dumpster-fire's kamikaze foreign-policy IEDs. See Luke McGee's January 13th, 2021, article *At the 11th Hour, Trump Hands Biden a Whole New Set of Foreign Policy Headaches* posted on cnn.com

https://www.cnn.com/2021/01/13/world/t
rump-biden-taiwan-cuba-yemen-
intl/index.html

– And Cathy Biank's November 30th, 2020, article *Trump is Openly Sabotaging Biden's Foreign Policy Before Leaving the White House* posted on worldnewsera.com

https://worldnewsera.com/news/trump-
is-openly-sabotaging-bidens-foreign-
policy-before-leaving-the-white-house/

[43] Notes for the Part Eight Epigraph:
"We cannot be satisfied until…" Harry S. Truman *Special Message to Congress,* reprinted in *Pegs to Hang Ideas on; a Book of Quotations* [Marjorie Weiser, Editor] (New York 1973), p. 103

https://archive.org/details/pegstohangide
aso0000weis/page/102/mode/2up

[44] Notes for Verse No. 47 (XLVII):
"Random acts of harshness pervade"

Vehicles used to attack people in crowds. See Hanna
Allam's June 21st, 2021, article *Vehicle Attacks Rise as
Extremists Target Protestors* posted on npr.org

https://www.npr.org/2020/06/21/880963
592/vehicle-attacks-rise-as-extremists-
target-protesters

– And Gop evilness apparently knows no bounds, for now
their Party seeks to make it legal in Gop-controlled states
to kill protestors with motor vehicles, as long as it's
against Pride Marches and Progressives causes. See
Cameron Peters' April 25th,

2021, article *Stave-Level Republicans Are Making it Easier to Run Over Protestors* posted on vox.com

https://www.vox.com/2021/4/25/223670
19/gop-laws-oklahoma-iowa-florida-
floyd-blm-protests-police

[45] Notes for Verse No. 48 (XLVIII):
"I want my dad!"

The very definition of brutal. See Marcia Greenwood / Will Cleveland / Brian Sharp's February 1st, 2021, article *Rochester, New York, Police Release Bodycam Video to Show Why Officers Were 'Required' to Handcuff, Pepper-Spray 9-Year-Old-Girl* reposted on usatoday.com

https://www.usatoday.com/story/news/n
ation/2021/01/31/rochester-police-
bodycam-videos-9-year-old-handcuffed-
pepper-sprayed/4333751001/

[46] Notes for Verse No. 49 (XLIX):
"Over the shoulder of Washington"

It was, I believe, also Franklin who later said the snake of slavery was coiled around the leg of Washington's desk, sleeping, but waiting to spread its venom through the newfound nation. For the rising / setting sun on the General's chair, see Lucy Davis' April 27th, 2015, article *Rising Sun Chair, Independence Hall* posted on philadelphiaencyclopedia.org

https://philadelphiaencyclopedia.org/me
diastream-1/

[47] Notes for Verse No. 50 (L):
"I read in the paper"

For how the effect the Rittenhouse excusal from justice affected Ahmaud Arbery's parents, see Tariro Mzezewa's November 23rd, 2021, article *The Arbery Family and*

Friends Say They Are Anxious But Hopeful of Guilty Verdicts posted on nytimes.com

https://www.nytimes.com/2021/11/23/us/
arbery-family-verdict-expectations.html

[48] Notes for Verse No. 52 (LII): Say Their Names II "Harum-Scarum backlash"

This is a reprint of Poem No. 41 (XLI) from AC Benus *Summer 2020 – Hell in a Handbasket* (San Francisco 2020). The 2021 update includes confirmation on the lawlessness within the L.A. County Sheriff's Office. See Tim Dickinson's September 14th, 2021, article *'Executioners,' 'Reapers,' and 'Banditos': Gangs of Sheriff's Deputies Are Wreaking Havoc in L.A.* posted on rollingstone.com

https://www.rollingstone.com/politics/poli
tics-news/los-angeles-sheriffs-
department-gangs-rand-report-1225982/

– And see Josh Cain's September 23rd, 2021, article *Despite Rand Report Showing Subgroups Are Common, L.A. County Sheriff Disputes Claims Deputy-Led Gangs Are Still Active* reposted on mercurynews.com

https://www.mercurynews.com/2021/09/
23/despite-rand-report-showing-
subgroups-are-common-la-countys-
sheriff-disputes-claims-deputy-led-
gangs-are-still-active/

– Also see the original notes for the poem in *Summer 2020 – Hell in a Handbasket*

[49] Notes for the Part Nine Epigraph:
"America today stands poised on a pinnacle of wealth and power" Stewart Udall *The Quiet Crisis,* reprinted in *Pegs to Hang Ideas on; a Book of Quotations* [Marjorie Weiser, Editor] (New York 1973), ps. 248-249

https://archive.org/details/pegstohangide
aso0000weis/page/248/mode/2up

[50] Notes for Verse No. 54 (LIV): Roundel
"Such good news"

Deadly smog in New Delhi. See Rajesh Kumar Singh's
January 10th, 2022, article *India's Deadly Air Pollution
Keeps Getting Worse, Not Better* posted on bloomberg.com

https://www.bloomberg.com/news/article
s/2022-01-11/india-s-deadly-air-
pollution-keeps-getting-worse-not-better

Tidewater sharks. See Amy Woodyatt's November 10th,
2021, article *Venomous Sharks Found in London's Thames
River* posted on cnn.com

https://www.cnn.com/travel/article/veno
mous-sharks-london-scli-intl-gbr-
scn/index.html

[51] Notes for Verse No. 55 (LV): The New Normal
"The New Norm, which we've yet to see"

Business-as-usual model will usher in a new Dark Age. See
Nafeez Ahmed's July 14th, 2021, article *MIT Predicted in
1972 that Society Will Collapse this Century: New Research
Shows We're on Schedule* posted on vice.com

https://www.vice.com/en/article/z3xw3x/
new-research-vindicates-1972-mit-
prediction-that-society-will-collapse-
soon

[52] Notes for Verse No. 56 (LVI): *von* Das letzte Lied
"Fern ab am Horizont, auf Felsenrissen"

Translation from Heinrich von Kleist's 1809 *The Final Number.* See the Meine Bibliothek entry posted on zeno.org

http://www.zeno.org/Literatur/M/Kleist,+
Heinrich+von/Gedichte/Gedichte/Das+le
tzte+Lied

[53] Notes for Verse No. 57 (LVII):
"What do you think can explain the mindset"

Our kids swimming in DDT. See CBS / The Associated Press' April 28th, 2021, article *"Staggering": 25,000 Barrels Found at Toxic Dump Site in Pacific Ocean off Los Angeles Coast* posted on cbsnews.com

https://www.cbsnews.com/news/ddt-barrels-toxic-waste-dump-pacific-ocean-california/

King Bush I's order to poison "our troops" rather than let the EPA do the clean-up on military bases. See Mary Manning / Rachael Levy's August 8th, 1996, article *Feds Investigating Burning of Hazardous Waste at Area 51* posted on lasvegassun.com

https://lasvegassun.com/news/1996/aug/08/feds-investigating-burning-of-hazardous-waste-at-a/

[54] Notes for Verse No. 58 (LVIII): Poisoned Blood "Not only COVID"

Prescription drugs in the water supply. See The Environmental Working Group's November, 2021, article *EPA Still Failing to Act on Widespread Toxic Chemicals Contamination of U.S. Drinking Water* posted on ewg.org

https://www.ewg.org/news-insights/news-release/2021/11/epa-still-failing-act-widespread-toxic-chemical-contamination-us

'Forever Chems' in human fetal blood. See The University of California's March 21st, 2021, article *Scientists Detect 55 Chemicals Never Before Reported in People – 42 "Mystery Chemicals" Whose Sources Are Unknown* reposted on scitechdaily.com

https://scitechdaily.com/scientists-detect-55-chemicals-never-before-reported-in-people-42-mystery-chemicals-whose-sources-are-unknown/

– And see Ashley Taylor's March 22nd, 2021, article *More Than 50 New Environmental Chemicals Detected in People: The Chemicals Were Discovered in a Study of Pregnant Women and their Newborns* posted on livescience.com

https://www.livescience.com/new-environmental-chemicals-pfas-pregnant-woment.html

[55] Notes for Verse No. 59 (LIX): Poisoned Air
"China's pollution now"

Unchecked environmental destruction. See Bloomberg News' May 6th, 2021, article *China's Emissions Now Exceed All the Developed World's Combined [Output]: China Spewed 27% of [Total] Global Greenhouse Gasses in 2019* posted on bloomberg.com

https://www.bloomberg.com/news/article
s/2021-05-06/china-s-emissions-now-
exceed-all-the-developed-world-s-
combined

[56] Notes for Verse No. 60 (LX): The Earth And Your Circadian Rhythms vs. The Military-Industrial Complex "We're so out of touch"

It's bad for us *(DUH!).* See Lindsay Kalter's November 5th, 2021, article *An Hour at What Cost? The Harmful Effects of Daylight Savings* posted on webmd.com

https://www.webmd.com/sleep-
disorders/news/20211105/harmful-
effects-of-daylight-savings

– And see Austin Lim's March 12th, 2021, article *The Dangers of Daylight Saving Time: It's Time to Do Away With a Time Adjustment that's Been Tied to Dire Health Consequences* posted on usnews.com

https://www.usnews.com/news/health-news/articles/2021-03-12/the-dangers-of-daylight-saving-time

[57] Notes for Verse No. 61 (LXI):
"In 2018, fossil fuel toxins"

Millions murdered outright by dino-juice poisons in the air every single year; year after year. See Oliver Milman's February 9th, 2021, article *'Invisible Killer': Fossil Fuels Caused 8.7 Million Deaths Globally in 2018, Research Finds* posted on theguardian.com

https://www.theguardian.com/environment/2021/feb/09/fossil-fuels-pollution-deaths-research

[58] Notes for Verse No. 62 (LXII):
"Who in the world today"

Self-reproducing Frankenbots. See Katie Hunt's November 29th, 2021, article *World's First Living Robots Now Reproduce, Scientists Say* posted on cnn.com

https://www.cnn.com/2021/11/29/americ as/xenobots-self-replicating-robots-scn/index.html

[59] Notes for the Part Ten Epigraph:
"The man who is swimming against the stream" Woodrow Wilson *The Harper Book of Quotations* [Robert Fitzhenry, Editor] (New York 1993), p. 15

https://archive.org/details/fitzhenrywhitesi 0000unse_p9g3/page/14/mode/2up

[60] Notes for Verse No. 63 (LXIII): Der höhere Frieden
"Wenn sich auf des Krieges Donnerwagen"

Translation of Heinrich von Kleist's 1792 *The Higher Peace.*
See the Meine Bibliothek entry posted on zeno.org

http://www.zeno.org/Literatur/M/Kleist,+
Heinrich+von/Gedichte/Gedichte/Der+h
%C3%B6here+Frieden

[61] Notes for Verse No. 64 (LXIV):
"The wicked Gop's Tiananmen Square"

December 2021 removal of last Tiananmen monuments from
Hong Kong. See Zen Soo's December 23rd, 2021, article
*Renowned Tiananmen Massacre Monument Removed in
Hong Kong* posted on apnews.com

https://apnews.com/article/china-beijing-
hong-kong-erosion-
288a06f7193356d6fcc671424a4446b6

– And see The Daily Mail's December 26th, 2021, article *Two More Statues Marking Tiananmen Square Massacre Are Torn Down as Crackdown on Dissent in Hong Kong Ramps Up* posted on dailymail.com

https://www.dailymail.co.uk/news/article-
10346487/Two-statues-marking-
Tiananmen-Square-massacre-torn-
down.html

– And see Hillary Leung's December 27th, 2021, article *Hong Kong's City University Demands Removal of Tiananmen Massacre Statue as Campus Crackdown Continues: Artwork that Pays Tribute to the 1989 Military Crackdown Are Being Torn Down Across University Campuses During the Festive Break, when Students Are Away* posted on hongkongfp.com

https://hongkongfp.com/2021/12/27/hong-kongs-city-university-demands-removal-of-tiananmen-massacre-statue-as-campus-crackdown-continues/

June 1989 reporting of executions. See Nicholas Kristof's June 22nd, 1989, article *Chinese Execute 3 in Public Display for Protest Role* posted on nytimes.com

https://www.nytimes.com/1989/06/22/world/chinese-execute-3-in-public-display-for-protest-role.html

Survivors' firsthand accounts. See Isabella Steger's May 6th, 2019, article *A Chinese Writer in Exile Chronicles the Lives of the "Thugs" who Survived Tiananmen Square in 1989* posted on qz.com

https://qz.com/1593708/bullets-and-opium-stories-of-surviving-tiananmen/

"The family of the victim is then sent a bill for 13 Chinese cents to cover the cost of the bullet." See The Orlando Sentinel's June 22nd, 2021, article *3 Executed as Chinese Defy West* posted on orlandosentinel.com

https://www.orlandosentinel.com/news/os-xpm-1989-06-22-8906230040-story.html

Gop co-opting of the Commie Party's "never happened" Big Lie. See Holmes Lybrand / Tera Subramaniam's July 27th, 2021, article *Fact Check: Some Republicans Have Tried to Rewrite the History of January 6. Here's How* posted on cnn.com

https://www.cnn.com/2021/07/27/politics
/republicans-rewrite-january-6-history-
fact-check/index.html

– And see The Associated Press' January 4th, 2022, article *Despite Brutal Video, Only GOP Minority Say [January 6th] Very Violent: A New Poll Shows that a Year After the Deadly Jan. 6 Insurrection at the U.S. Capitol, Only About 4 in 10 Republicans Recall the Attack by Supporters of then-President Donald Trump as Very Violent or Extremely Violent* reposted on usnews.com

https://www.usnews.com/news/politics/a
rticles/2022-01-04/less-than-half-of-gop-
say-1-6-was-very-violent-ap-norc-poll

[62] Notes for Verse No. 65 (LXV):
"Three hundred twenty-nine days"

The slaying of Mario Gonzalez. See Libby Cohen's April 28th, 2021, article *Video Shows Cops Kneeling on Man 5 Minutes Before He Died: The Video is Strikingly Similar to the Death of George Floyd* posted on dailydot.com

https://www.dailydot.com/debug/mario-gonzalez-george-floyd/

For the family denied access to justice, see Jason Green's April 20th, 2021, article *'Our Family Needs Answers': Relatives Call for Swift Transparence in Oakland Man's Death During Arrest by Alameda Police* posted on eastbaytimes.com

https://www.eastbaytimes.com/2021/04/
20/alameda-police-officers-did-not-use-
weapons-on-man-who-died-in-custody-
body-camera-footage-exists/

– And see Richard Winton's May 11th, 2021, article *Family Wants Federal Inquiry of Alameda Police in Death of Mario Gonzalez* posted on latimes.com

https://www.latimes.com/california/story/
2021-05-11/alameda-police-death-
mario-gonzalez

[63] Notes for Verse No. 66 (LXVI):
"What sadder lilac upon the threshold"

Second-opinion autopsy conducted by George Floyd's family. See the State of Minnesota's August 25th, 2020, District Court filing *Family Attorneys: Independent Autopsy Finds George Floyd Died from Asphyxia Due to Sustained Forceful Pressure* posted on mncourts.gov

https://mncourts.gov/mncourtsgov/medi
a/High-Profile-Cases/27-CR-20-12949-
TT/Exhibit608252020.pdf

[64] Notes for Verse No. 66 (LXVI):
"These victims of hallucinations"

Epistle of Jude to his partner James, brother of Jesus. For a
word by word breakdown of the Greek language original, see
the Bible Hub's interlinear *Jude*

https://biblehub.com/interlinear/jude/1.ht
m

[65] Notes for Verse No. 73 (LXXIII): Sonnet
"How long ago it feels our Nation had"

Franklin Delano Roosevelt's "Four Freedoms," something to which each person on Earth was entitled. See Roosevelt's January 6th, 1941, *State of the Union Address to Congress* posted on ourdocuments.gov

https://www.ourdocuments.gov/doc.php
?flash=false&doc=70&page=transcript

[66] Notes for Verse No. 74 (LXXIV): Too Little; Too Late
i. "What We Do Today"

An Aussie warren. See Eric Lutz's September 16th, 2019, article *James Murdoch Suggests His Dad's Empire is Ruining America: He "Really Disagrees" with the Views on Fox News* posted on vanityfair.com

https://www.vanityfair.com/news/2019/0
9/james-murdoch-fox-news-empire

ii. "The Environmental Economy"

General Motors' betrayal of the American consumer. See Hannah Lutz's April 18th, 2021, article *25 Years Ago, GM Rolled Out the EV1, a Triumph of Electrification that Ended in a Crushing Blow [to the Consumer]: Here's How Those Who Lived the EV1 Saga Remember It* posted on autonews.com

https://www.autonews.com/automakers-suppliers/heres-how-those-who-lived-ev1-saga-remember-it

– And "Eon Musk was really inspired by the EV1's sad end, as he stated about the origins of his company." See Aurelie Saboureau's 2019 article *The EV1: The Forgotten Tesla's Inspiration* posted on drivetribe.com

https://drivetribe.com/p/the-ev1-the-forgotten-teslas-inspiration-ER4574OZRjqR3UH5Tx9bMA?iid=GVw A6NtbQnmlkna-rpvp1w

The buying of California law. See Chris Pain's 2005 documentary film *Who Killed the Electric Car?* posted by Videojunk714's in full on youtube.com

https://www.youtube.com/watch?v=3fW 4xYBXdGo

Compare GM's sell-out of democracy versus the worldwide domination of the Toyota vehicle developed for the exact same California regulation Detroit paid to have killed. See Stephen Edelstein's April 28th, 2020, article *Toyota Has Sold More Than 15 Million Hybrids Globally* posted on greencarreports.com

https://www.greencarreports.com/news/
1127969_toyota-has-sold-more-than-15-
million-hybrids-globally

– And see Matthew DeBord's June 19th, 2018, article *The Toyota Prius Is One of the Most Important Cars of the Past 20 Years – Here's a Look at Its Impressive History* posted on businessinsider.com

https://www.businessinsider.com/toyota-
prius-is-most-important-car-last-20-
years-2017-12

iii. "Myth-Making Politics"

The militarization of community law forces. See Wayne McElrath / Sarah Tuberville's June 9th, 2020, article *Poisoning Our Police: How the Militarization Mindset Threatens Constitutional Rights and Public Safety* posted on pogo.org

https://www.pogo.org/analysis/2020/06/
poisoning-our-police-how-the-
militarization-mindset-threatens-
constitutional-rights-and-public-safety/

– And see Charlotte Lawrence / Cyrus O'Brien / Maritza Perez's May 12th, 2021, article *It's Past Time to End the Federal Militarization of Police: Our New Report Documents the Critical Need to Repeal 1033, which Allows the Federal Government to Equip Local Police with Military Gear* posted on aclu.org

https://www.aclu.org/news/civil-
liberties/its-past-time-to-end-the-federal-
militarization-of-police/

The NRA's double-down on mass murder. See Everytown's November 9th, 2021, press release *Bombshell: Secret Tape Reveals NRA's Internal Response to Columbine School Shooting. Report Shows NRA Only Cared About Self-Preservation; Called Own Members "Hillbillies"* posted on everytown.org

https://www.everytown.org/press/bombs hell-secret-tape-reveals-nras-internal-response-to-columbine-school-shooting/

– And see the Saint Louis Post-Dispatch's Editorial Board's November 9th, 2021, article *Editorial: How the NRA Used the Columbine Massacre to Make Gun Control the Enemy* posted on stltoday.com

https://www.stltoday.com/opinion/editori
al/editorial-how-the-nra-used-the-
columbine-massacre-to-make-gun-
control-the-enemy/article_e8f94099-
147b-5c56-adcd-8259514f1de5.html

iv. "Forgive me" – Social Justice

A laughable 'development'; meanwhile, Toyota became the United States' No. 1 automaker in 2021 with little fanfare. See [if you can read it with a straight face] Paul Eisenstein's January 28th, 2021, article *GM To Go All-Electric by 2035; Phase Out Gas and Diesel Engines* posted on nbcnews.com

https://www.nbcnews.com/business/aut
os/gm-go-all-electric-2035-phase-out-
gas-diesel-engines-n1256055

[67] Notes for the Epilogue: A last plea from the last day of the year
"I think of him there"

Separate and unequal sleeping arrangements. See Newstalk Newsroom's October 24th, 2020, article *Life in Donald Trump's White House: Separate Bedrooms and*

Scared Staff: Staff in White House Are "Very Afraid" to Speak Out Under the Presidency of Dondald Trump posted on newstalk.com

https://www.newstalk.com/news/life-donald-trumps-white-house-separate-bedrooms-scared-staff-1095647

– And see Ellen Cranley's December 3rd, 2019, article *Melania Trump Sleeps in Her Own Room on a Separate Floor Away from the President, According to New Book* posted on buisinessinsider.com

https://www.businessinsider.com/melania-trump-separate-room-separate-floor-white-house-2019-12

– And see Diane Herbst's May 10th, 2018, article *Melania and Donald Trump Are the Rare – But Not*

ONLY – Presidential Couple to Use Separate Bedrooms…an Arrangement the Country Hasn't Seen in More Than Forty Years posted on people.com

https://people.com/politics/melania-donald-trump-separate-bedrooms-historical-perspective/

It ain't Diet Coke, kiddies . . . . See Howard Dean's September 27th, 2016, appearance on *The Showdown,* in a segment entitled "Howard Dean Stands by Cocaine Tweet about Donald Trump" posted by MSNBC on youtube.com

https://www.youtube.com/watch?v=EfY8 0rWaeCU

Lincoln's ghost in general. See Katherine Brodt's October 29th, 2020, article *The Legends of Lincoln's Ghost* posted on boundarystones.weta.org

https://boundarystones.weta.org/2020/1
0/29/legends-lincolns-ghost

– And see Theresa Vargas' October 30th, 2017, article *Is the White House Haunted? A History of Spooked Presidents, Prime Ministers and Pets* posted on washingtonpost.com

https://www.washingtonpost.com/news/r
etropolis/wp/2017/10/30/is-the-white-
house-haunted-a-history-of-spooked-
presidents-prime-ministers-and-pets/

– And see Dora Mekouar's October 31st, 2020, article *Is the White House Haunted?* posed on voanews.com

https://www.voanews.com/a/usa_all-about-america_white-house-haunted/6197647.html

– And see Justin Vallejo's April 27th, 2021, article *"Maybe It's President Lincoln's Ghost": Jen Psaki Press Briefing Interrupted by Curious Creaking Sounds* posted on independent.co.uk

https://www.independent.co.uk/news/wo
rld/americas/us-politics/jen-psaki-
abraham-lincoln-ghost-b1838574.html

~

www.ingramcontent.com/pod-product-compliance
Lightning Source LLC
Chambersburg PA
CBHW031955040426
42448CB00006B/369